ONE MORE CHANCE

A True Story of Survival and Faith

KIDNAPPED AND HELD FOR RANSOM

ONE MORE CHANCE

ROBERT MEEK
WITH ALLAN WEBB

A True Story of Survival and Faith

Editorial work and production management by Eschler Editing
Interior print design and layout by Sydnee Hyer
eBook design and layout by Sydnee Hyer

Published by Scrivener Books

First Edition: June 2019

ISBN: 978-1-949165-13-5

CONTENTS

ACKNOWLEDGMENTS

ROBERT MEEK

I WOULD LIKE TO THANK MY WIFE, LYNETTE, for her love and commitment and for encouraging me to share my story. I am also indebted to my children and their spouses for their encouragement. I am grateful for the love and support of my colleagues and for their willingness to share this story from their point of view. I must also express my appreciation for all those who prayed for my release while I was held captive. I know it was the power of those prayers that led to my release, and I will never be able to adequately thank them for that. Over the last couple years, I have had the opportunity to share my experience with literally thousands. I share my gratitude with them for encouraging me to undertake this project. Finally, I appreciate Falon Brawley, for the cover design.

ALLAN WEBB

SHARING SOMEONE ELSE'S STORY, IN THEIR VOICE, is a monumental task. I express gratitude to my wife for encouraging me to contact Bob Meek in the first place and for being by my side throughout the process. I appreciate Bob for having the confidence to let me tell his story. I was moved by it, as I'm sure you will be, and it was humbling to be part of helping him get this out to the world. I am grateful to Jamie Ellison and Sarah Butikofer for providing key insights as we went along and for making sure I stayed true to the story. Katie Stirling, of Eschler Editing, provided incredible insight as editor, and the story flows far better due to her thorough but respectful editing. Finally, I am grateful to parents who constantly told me I could do anything I wanted if I set my mind to it. That has turned out to be far more true in my life than I ever imagined.

PREFACE

IT'S BEEN WITH SOME TREPIDATION THAT I SHARE with the world the most traumatic experience of my life. In fact, it's been more than two years since it happened, and it's fairly recently that I've felt like I could put it out there in a book. It's not that I'm afraid to share it. Nor am I ashamed of any aspect of it. It's simply that this was such a profound—almost sacred—experience, I have wondered whether it's even appropriate to share widely. Obviously, I've decided that it is and that now is the time. I hope you find it useful in some way.

My purpose in sharing is not just to simply satisfy the curiosity of those who would find entertainment in such things. My sincere hope (and really the only reason I have chosen to share) is that it will be beneficial to someone I've never met. And I don't mean beneficial to someone who travels to Mexico on business. I truly hope to reach people on a much deeper, more fundamental level. If you come to the end of this book and look deep into your own soul, then I've accomplished what I set out to do.

I think when we read about things that happen to people, whether it be accident, disease, catastrophe, heroic or horrific things, or even tremendously joyous things, we have a tendency to think, "Oh yes—but that person is larger (or perhaps smaller) than life. They're somehow different than I am." But what I've learned from having spoken with many people who've had those types of experiences is they're just regular people—ordinary people who have undergone an extraordinary experience, for better or worse.

Well, that's my situation. I had an extraordinary experience, to be sure, but I can assure you there is nothing extraordinary about me.

Anytime you undertake the task of relating an experience like this, there are certain risks. I suppose the first risk is that of inaccuracy. Over time, the memory of what happened naturally fades. That's just human frailty, and there is no way around it. That said, however, this experience has been burned so deeply into my mind I'm not sure I can ever forget it—even those parts that would, perhaps, be better forgotten. If there are any inaccuracies in this story, they are not intentional, and they would relate to minor details, such as the sequencing of what happened, and not to the substance of what happened. I have taken great care to assure that what I've related in the story is as factual and as accurate as I can possibly make it.

Second, there's a risk of inadvertently putting someone I care deeply about in harm's way. Quite frankly, that has been my biggest concern in sharing my story. The more truthfully and factually I tell the story, the more some of the people involved will be placed at risk. For that reason, of necessity, I have changed the names of some of the people involved, as well as altering small details sufficiently to protect their anonymity. The changes I've made don't change the story, they simply had to be made so that I could tell my story in good conscience.

Finally, there's a risk that people might misconstrue what I've said and why I've said it. You can't live your life worried about what other people do or don't think, but I feel the burden of telling the story in a way that reaches people in the way I intended to reach them. I have done my very best to do that, and only time will tell if I've been successful.

I have been careful not to "overtell" the story. I have not sensationalized the details to make it read better. On the other hand, many of the threats made to me were so vile and so graphic I chose to refer to them generally instead of spelling them out word for word. Doing this doesn't change the story; it simply makes it more palatable.

With those things in mind, I invite you to settle in, buckle up, and prepare for the ride of your life. If I were going to offer suggestions on how to read this book, I would say it's better read in big chunks. Many people have read it one or two sittings. You'll figure out what works best for you. However you read it, I hope you find it thought-provoking. Enjoy!

CHAPTER ONE

BEGINNING OF THE NIGHT OF TERROR

THURSDAY
9:00 P.M.
WYNDHAM HOTEL
CHIHUAHUA, MEXICO

THE JANGLING OF THE HOTEL TELEPHONE forced its way into the tranquility of the room like a battering ram in the hands of a SWAT team. It had been so quiet and peaceful, and I had been so absorbed with answering all my correspondence, that the bell made me jerk up so quickly I nearly fell off the bed. It was more than just being startled—way more. I felt a chill run up my spine. Call it intuition, call it a premonition, call it whatever you want—something wasn't right about that phone ringing. It's like walking into a place you've never been before and yet, somehow, you know things aren't exactly as they should be.

That's what this phone call, unbidden and, quite frankly, unwanted, did for me. My mind froze for an instant. All I could do in that moment was just sit and stare at the phone as I tried to sort through it. Who did I know who knew I was at this hotel? More importantly, who did I know who knew I was at this hotel who didn't already have my cell phone number? Why would someone call the hotel instead of calling me directly on my cell? A million questions and a rapidly growing sense of uneasiness began to invade my consciousness as I stood to answer the phone.

As I walked over to the desk where the phone was located, the idea crossed my mind that this was a middle-of-the-night call. Good news never comes in the middle of the night. Nobody calls you at 3:00 a.m. to tell you they're having a great day or that you've just won the lottery. No. Calls in the middle of the night invariably bring bad news. This call wasn't in the middle of the night. It was only 9:00 p.m., but it held the same unexplainable dread of a call coming much later.

As I answered the phone, what I heard from the voice on the other end made my blood run cold. "Señor Meek, this is hotel security. We regret to inform you that the hotel is under siege from two rival cartels. They are going room to room searching, and people are being killed in their rooms as we speak. If you'll stay on the phone with me and give me the information I need, we're going to do everything we can to keep you safe."

If people are being shot, I've got to protect myself from stray bullets, I thought. I immediately thought of going to the bathroom, thinking it would be safer to lie down inside an iron bathtub. But as I thought about the tub, I realized it wasn't really deep enough to provide any real protection, and the fact that it was separated from the hallway by only a thin wall made me re-think my plan.

I went back to the bed and looked around. The room had a bed and nightstand in one end and a couch and desk in the other end. The two parts of the room were separated by a four-foot-high wooden divider. I decided the safest place to be was on the floor between the bed and the wooden divider. I lay flat on the floor, wondering when bullets would begin ripping through the walls of my room.

It's interesting how your mind works in adrenaline-charged situations. In a tenth of the time it takes to blink your eye, you see an entire scene from your past that may have taken hours—or even days to unfold—replayed on the screen of your mind as though it were in real time. This was one of those situations for me.

While serving as a missionary in Guatemala in the early eighties, we got a call from our mission president late one night instructing us to visit the family of a sick missionary to let them know of their son's condition. We had driven out to a small village to explain what was going on and were returning to our apartment around midnight.

The eighties were a turbulent time in Guatemala, and there were armed guerilla factions everywhere disrupting everything. For this reason, traveling at night was only undertaken in the most dire circumstances.

As we came around the corner of the dirt road outside that village, the road was blocked by two large military-style trucks. Armed men were everywhere on the road. It was too narrow to turn around, and there was not time to do anything but stop and be interrogated.

It was one of the first of a handful of experiences I have had in my life where if you panic and do or say the wrong thing it could cost you your life. So rather than appear like I had something to hide, I drove right up to the man with the machine gun and rolled down my window.

"Good evening, sir," I said in Spanish.

"Good evening," he replied, tersely. "Who are you and where are you going?"

"We are missionaries from The Church of Jesus Christ," I replied as cheerfully as I could muster.

"We were given the assignment to tell a sick missionary's family about his situation and are just heading home."

This hard-bitten guerilla on the other end of the gun looked right through me for several seconds. About the time I felt I'd made a huge mistake in being so bold, he waved his hand at the driver of one of the trucks to move it out of the way for us.

"Get out of here," he commanded. "And don't come back here like this again."

I assured him we wouldn't be back and drove on. In some small way, that experience and others like it prepared me for what was happening now. Even though alarms were blaring out their warning in my mind, and even though my blood had been replaced with pure adrenaline, I knew the only way I would ever find my way out of this situation was to keep my head. One bad decision, one wrong word, one error of any kind, could be my last. I had to force down the fear, calm my nerves, and respond more rationally than I really felt.

But although previous experiences had helped prepare me in some ways for this situation, I knew this was different. This wasn't just the adrenaline that sharpens your senses and increases your focus. This was fear, and even as I say that, I almost have to laugh. Fear is something that comes from things that go bump in the night. This was so far beyond fear that even using that word seems absurd.

The only problem is there isn't another word. Terror, maybe. Horror? I can't come up with just the right word or phrase that adequately describes how I felt. Yes, I was afraid. Yes, I was terrified. Yes, I thought it was very possible I was going to die. Yes, I was desperately concerned for my wife and loved ones back in the States.

That fear, that terror, was now growing inside me at an alarming rate—preparing to consume me. I felt like the pressure from the inside was going to crush my windpipe or squeeze my heart so intensely it would cease beating. It was a deep, primal fear. The kind that comes from the deepest recesses of what psychologists call the lizard brain—that fundamental and all-powerful mechanism of self-preservation. It is fear that comes from a level so deep, many people—perhaps most people—will never see it manifested in their lifetime.

While I had been searching for the safest place in the room, I continued on the telephone with the man from hotel security. He was asking all kinds of questions. He wanted to know who I was, what I was doing in Chihuahua, what company I was with, how long I had been in Mexico, what I had been doing in my time there, etc. Then he started asking about my home and my family.

Those questions caused my racing mind to jump to my wife and children. Would I see them again? Would I feel the tender embrace of the incredible woman I had loved so completely for thirty-one wonderful years? Would I be there for grandchildren to leap into my lap? Would I be there to offer advice to my children as they stood at the crossroads of life? So many questions. So few answers.

I have been blessed with a very close-knit family. We play together, we work together, we worship together—we do everything together. My mind drifted to evenings on the lake. We spent summers waterskiing and winters snow skiing. If we weren't working, we were playing. I wondered whether they would be playing without me in the future. The thought was almost too much to bear.

I've traveled both internationally and domestically enough to know that you don't unnecessarily divulge personal information about yourself or your situation with strangers. So when the hotel clerk asked about the family, red flag immediately went up. But then again, this wasn't a stranger. He was from hotel security. His role in this whole thing was to keep me safe. My world was about to come completely unraveled, and this was the only person between me and the unravelling. I could trust him. He said so. And I didn't really have any other choice.

We stayed on the phone for what seemed like an eternity. But it was actually probably only ten to fifteen minutes. After he had gathered all the information he could, he asked one last question: "Mr. Meek, do you have a cell phone?" I told him I did, and he said, "Give me the number to your cell phone so if they take out our phone system I can call you."

Looking back now, that seems odd. He had just called me on the house phone to warn me about the cartel's actions. Why did he think they would take out the house phone system? Somehow it all didn't sit right with me, but at the time, I had no reason to doubt anything he said. He was my friend, and he was going to keep me safe. If that's what he needed to keep me safe, I would, and did, give my cell number to him—no questions asked.

We said our goodbyes, and I hung up. I lay on the floor staring up at the ceiling, wondering what had happened. The fear flowed through my body like high-voltage electricity. My mind raced wildly out of control.

I wondered if I would get out of Mexico alive. I'd heard horrific tales of the cartels and their ruthless—almost inhuman—activities. I'd seen the pictures of the disembodied heads hung from Mexican bridges or on a pike at the side of the road. A deep, penetrating shudder went through my body as I pictured my own head next to those.

I was jolted out of my macabre reverie by the sound of the ringer on my cell phone. I looked down to see a number I didn't recognize, and my first thought was to ignore it. But then I realized it was probably security with information I needed to have.

I answered the phone, not having any idea that what had become my worst nightmare had been—at most—a lukewarm prelude to what was coming.

CHAPTER TWO

PRODUCE BUSINESS

SIX MONTHS EARLIER

AFTER GROWING UP IN THE POTATO SHEDS of Southern Colorado and enjoying my time in the produce business, I decided to stick with it for a career. I had a talent for it, and I enjoyed it. In pretty much every way, it has been a perfect fit in my life.

At the age of nineteen, I served a two-year mission for my church in Guatemala, where I learned to speak fluent Spanish, which has turned out to be a huge benefit to me in being able to communicate with people in all aspects of the business. I've used the Spanish I learned almost daily in my career, talking to growers, farm workers, factory workers, and our many customers in Spanish-speaking countries. In fact, it's hard to imagine how I would have been able to accomplish what I have without being able to speak Spanish.

The first thing you learn in the produce business is that it's seasonal in nature. You plant in the spring, you harvest in the late summer to early fall, and, where appropriate, you put the product in cold storage and sell as long as the product lasts. But the reality is, it's a perishable product and doesn't last forever. That means there's a period (usually several months) when various types of produce are difficult, if not impossible, to find.

For that reason, many produce marketers have turned to Mexico and other Latin American countries to solve that problem. Because their growing seasons are different from ours, they will still have fresh produce for sale when sources in the United States are drying up. It has been this desire to make fresh, wholesome food available to people everywhere that has driven me to find sources of high-quality produce in Mexico.

I don't think there has been a year in the last fifteen that I haven't been in Mexico or some other country in Latin America at least once to meet with growers, attend a trade show or expo, or just to stay abreast of what was happening in agriculture there. Latin America is the key to year-round availability of fresh food, and my colleagues and I have come to count on Mexican growers.

So it was no surprise when I received a call from an onion grower in Mexico named Pablo. Pablo indicated he had a substantial onion operation in the Mexican state of Chihuahua. I was immediately interested. We were already working with growers in the eastern part of Mexico, but because the growing seasons change from east to west and from north to south, having a grower as far west as Chihuahua would fill in another gap in the fresh-food chain.

My good friend and colleague Shawn and I met Pablo a few weeks later at an expo in Mexico City. He was a likeable person and one of those people you just know you would be happy doing business with. We were looking forward to getting to know him better.

After returning from Mexico City, we continued our relationship with Pablo by telephone. It wasn't long before Pablo and his sales manager came to Utah to have a look at our operation. That's the way business is done all over the world. You meet someone, and if there's chemistry, you go to the next step. That next step is going to visit the person and see if their company is legitimate. That's why Pablo was in Utah, and that's why he invited us to come to Mexico.

We had a good meeting with Pablo and his sales manager, but when he invited us to come to Northern Mexico, we expressed some concern over safety. We have an office in McAllen, Texas, and our managers there hadn't actually visited Mexico for several years because of the danger. Pablo assured us that Chihuahua wasn't as dangerous as everyone said and that he would care for us from the time we got there until the time we left.

My partner wasn't convinced that Pablo would be able to keep us safe, but having traveled so extensively in Mexico, I felt like we would be fine if we made the trip. Most people who get into trouble traveling internationally do so going to bars and nightclubs or being out and about late at night. I have never been one to go to bars or nightclubs, and there is no reason for me to be out late in the evening.

Of course, I have always taken many other precautions that have kept me safe. I learned as a missionary that you're safer if you blend in. I have never dressed in flashy clothing when I'm traveling, and I haven't worn expensive watches and rings. I've just tried to blend in. I've also made it a point to be aware of my surroundings. I've always watched what other people are doing and how they're acting. If you listen to stories of people who travel extensively internationally, you'll realize you're much safer if you take on this heightened sense of awareness before you get to your destination and don't put it down until you're back home. These things are true for travel anywhere, but they're especially true internationally. I've always taken these precautions as if they were the rules of the game, and I have been successful following them for decades of international travel. I have learned from years of experience how to keep myself safe, and I never let down my guard—not even for a minute.

Another thing that gave me an additional sense of security is my ability to talk to people and find common ground with them. I can converse as comfortably in Spanish as in English. I have worked in sales and negotiation my whole career, and it's very rare for me to find someone with whom I'm unable to find common ground. It's rare for me to have an adversarial relationship with anyone.

I felt I understood the danger in Mexico, and I felt like doing those things in my power to protect myself—as well as having Pablo's help as a local—meant the danger wasn't really significant enough for me to be overly concerned.

We concluded Pablo's visit to our office in Utah and decided I would find a time that was a good fit for all of us and we'd eventually come for a visit.

Normally, things like that are planned well in advance, but this time it was different. A few weeks later, I was in Dallas doing some work with our office there and unexpectedly finished a couple days early. Normally, both Shawn and I would have gone to visit the grower, but I was only two hours from Chihuahua by plane, and the timing couldn't have been better. It was September of 2016, and Pablo was right in the middle of his harvest. It was a perfect time for a visit. I decided to call him and arrange to tour his operation in Mexico. He was available, and that evening I was on a plane.

Shawn was concerned about my visit to Chihuahua when I called him to tell him what I was going to do.

"I don't care what Pablo says," he stated. "I've seen the news. I know what happens to people in that area. I'm just not comfortable with you going."

"I'm not moving there," I told him cheerfully. "I'll be in and out before anyone even knows I'm there. I'll arrive tonight, we'll look at his operation tomorrow, and I'll be out of there early the next morning."

The last thing Shawn said to me before I left for Mexico was, "Be careful. It's not safe there." He had no idea how prophetic that statement would turn out to be.

CHAPTER THREE

ARRIVING IN MEXICO

11:00 P.M.
WEDNESDAY NIGHT
CHIHUAHUA, MEXICO

I ARRIVED IN CHIHUAHUA AT ABOUT 11:00 P.M. LOCAL TIME. It would have been safer to arrive in the morning, but after Pablo's assurances, I wasn't too concerned, and I wanted to maximize my time there. Arriving in the morning would have killed the whole day—a day I didn't have to waste. When I told Pablo I was coming, he asked if I wanted him to meet me at the airport. He lived far from Chihuahua, and I didn't want to put him out. I told him I'd take a taxi to the hotel and he could pick me up in the morning.

While on the plane, I'd had a marvelous discussion with a Mexican businessman named Alvaro, who spent part of his time in Texas and part of his time in Chihuahua.

"What brings you to Mexico?" he asked.

"I'm in the produce business," I replied. "I'm meeting with a grower in your area who will hopefully be able to provide onions for the US market," I replied. "We work with several growers here in Mexico and are always looking for new ones."

"Why Mexico?" Alvaro asked.

"The growing seasons here are different from those in the United States. You have a crop here that is harvested in June through August. Our crop is harvested and packed September through May. By buying onions in Mexico, we've effectively lengthened the time our customers can buy fresh produce by four months. It's a win-win. Your growers have a larger market for their produce, and our customers get fresh produce for more of the year. It's makes perfect sense to buy here."

We continued conversing for the two-hour trip from Dallas to Chihuahua. By the time we got there, it seemed like we'd known each other much longer than two hours. Alvaro was comfortable to talk with, and I enjoyed his company.

When we landed, he suggested we share a taxi into town, and I agreed. We dropped him off at his destination, and the taxi took me to the Wyndham Suites hotel. I had a great conversation in Spanish with the young man at the desk as I checked in, and there was nothing out of the ordinary.

As is the case in Mexico and in most international destinations, really, before you can get a room, you have to fill out a form telling them everything there is to know about you. They want to know why you're there, how long you're staying, what you'll be doing while you're there, etc. They also want a copy of your passport, your email address, home address, etc. It's a huge data breach, but if you're going to get a room, you have to provide it.

After a short night, Pablo picked me up at the hotel first thing the next morning. We drove and drove to get to his farm. The roads went from wide two-lane highways to narrow, two-lane paved roads, to dirt roads, and finally to what most people would call a trail. I wondered how in the world they got semis in and out of there.

The state of Chihuahua is basically one big desert. There is lava rock, sagebrush, cactus, and that's about it. It's always a surprise when you drive for hours in the most desolate desert only to round a corner and find yourself in a Shangri-La with beautiful, verdant agricultural fields as far as the eye can see. And yet one minute before, all you could see was sagebrush. It never ceases to amaze me. Mexico has awesome farmland. It needs to be irrigated to be able to produce, but the ground itself is great for most crops.

We spent a couple hours driving around the farm, talking about differences in harvesting in Mexico and the United States. He showed me their packing plant. In the United States, we harvest the product and take it to a packing plant in town where the product is sorted for size and put into bags for retail sale. In Mexico, at least at the bigger operations, these things are done right on the farm. When product is loaded on a truck and headed for market, they don't make any additional stops until they get there. Everything on the truck has already been sorted, packaged, and is ready to sell.

Pablo's operation was everything he had said it was and more. It was run like a large operation in the United States, and the product was first-rate. I came away impressed with what I saw and ready to market his product in the States.

We left the farm and made the long drive back to Chihuahua. Our conversations throughout the day had largely focused on business and the business relationship we were trying to forge through the visit he had made to our facilities and now through my visit to his.

We arrived in Chihuahua about 4:30 p.m. Thursday afternoon and opted for an early dinner. As it often does, the conversation over dinner shifted from business to our personal lives. It was one of those conversations people have when they're trying to find enough commonality on which to form the foundation of a business deal. We talked about common acquaintances in the business, interesting experiences we'd each had—we even touched on religion and politics deeply enough to be assured there were no hidden challenges there—and then the conversation turned to family.

"Tell me about your family," Pablo said.

"You might not want to get me started on my family," I told him smiling. "Once I get started, it's hard for me to stop."

I went on to explain how my wife and I had met and how I knew I should marry her, even though I was engaged to be married to another woman in just a few short weeks. I told him about my children and how fortunate we were to be close enough that we enjoyed doing everything together.

"How about you?" I asked. "Is your family close?"

"Well," he said as he leaned back with a big smile on his face. "You know Mexico is very Catholic and as such is very family oriented. Like you, my wife and I have placed a high priority on our family. Fortunately, we too have been blessed by strong family relationships and children who love each other and who love us."

Something about the conversation just felt completely right. I knew we would do business for a long time with Pablo. And even more importantly, I knew he would be someone we could trust as we went forward. By the time we finished eating, we were both ready to work closely together. It had been a fruitful trip.

We finished dinner about 6:00 p.m., and Pablo asked if I'd like him to accompany me to the hotel or take me to the airport in the morning. I told him I was going to go to the mall across the street from the hotel to look around and that I'd get a taxi in the morning, as I had an early flight. We said our goodbyes, and that was the last time I saw him.

I wandered aimlessly through the mall for an hour or so. I'm not a shopper, but sometimes it seems like I think better when I'm moving. I grew up like more than half of American children did. I was born and raised in a small, rural community in Southwest Colorado. I had all the experiences you have when you grow up in a small town.

My father was what the world would call a traveling salesman and, as such, was seldom home. And when I say seldom, I mean he was home about four to five nights a month. As is often the case, the pressures of two married people living what amounted to separate lives eventually led to a breakdown in my parents' marriage.

I was twelve when they divorced. It was a hard for me but not unexpected. For most of my life, my father had been absent. And because of that, as the oldest son, I took on the role as "man of the house." Even as a young boy, I did many of the things a husband or father would do around the house.

Growing up, it seemed I was constantly busy with school, chores, and everything else I need to help with to keep the household running. There was precious little time for "sitting around," and I became accustomed to being busy. I learned to ponder and daydream while I was on the move. So I walked around the mall and pondered the events of the day. I was pleased I had come.

About 7:00 p.m. I headed back over to the hotel to settle in for the night. I made a Skype call to my wife, who was in Idaho visiting our children who lived there, and we spoke for a while. Then I started in on responding to the emails I'd received during the last couple days. I was in the middle of that when the house phone rang. Little did I know that call would be the beginning of an eighteen-hour descent into the darkest depths of hell.

CHAPTER FOUR

THE CARTEL

9:15 P.M.
THURSDAY EVENING
WYNDHAM HOTEL
CHIHUAHUA, MEXICO

THE VOICE ON MY CELL PHONE WAS THE SAME VOICE I had just been speaking to for the last fifteen minutes. But now the tone had changed, like watching the fog roll in on the coast. You can see it coming and the next thing you know, you're enveloped in the fog and can't see anything. A wave of cold, wet, inky-black darkness settled in around me at the sound of his voice.

If someone asked me to paint a picture of evil, I wouldn't know how to do that. But the voice on the other end of the line was sinister—darker than anything I had ever heard. It was pure evil—an evil I could feel howling into the depths of my very soul. And the words spoken confirmed with alarming intensity the feelings of evil I had been experiencing.

"Señor Meek, this is"—he gave me his name, but I honestly can't remember what it was—"and I represent the cartel called La Linea Juarez. We are the most ruthless cartel in all of Mexico, and you will do exactly as we say."

Talk about being sucker punched. The air rushed out of my lungs, and I began to wonder if my legs would continue to support me. This man who just minutes before had been my lifeline—someone in hotel security whose responsibility it was to keep me safe—was telling me that not only was he not security, he was now my captor.

"Listen to me very carefully," this intensely menacing voice on the other end of the line said. "If you make one mistake, you will be killed. The hotel is completely under our control. We have people in the hallways. We have people in the stairwells. We have people outside the building right now, and all of them are carefully watching your room to make sure you don't make any attempt to leave. We have all of your electronic devices bugged. If you try to send a text or an email or in any other way attempt to contact anyone outside this room, or if you leave the room by any means, or if you break the connection on this call, we will kill you immediately. If you do everything we say, and do it exactly as you're instructed, you will be okay. But never forget, if you make one wrong move, we will kill you." I was reeling. Seeking some sort of shelter, I again lay down between the bed and the half wall that separated the sleeping area from the sitting area, somehow hoping against hope that would keep me safe.

I lay there on my back, staring up at the ceiling of a second-rate Mexican hotel, wondering what in the world was going on. Intellectually, I understood everything I was being told, but emotionally I couldn't (or wouldn't) accept it. My thoughts were racing completely out of control. Surely this couldn't be happening. I must have fallen asleep and this must be a horrible, bad dream. Somebody needed to pinch me. Somehow I needed to wake up. Just twenty minutes ago I had been Skyping my wife, who was visiting our children in Idaho, and all was right with the world. Now I was—emotionally, at least—being shaken like a rag doll in the mouth of an angry pit bull, fighting for my life against the "most ruthless cartel" in all of Mexico.

But it wasn't a dream. It was real—all too real. I was being held captive against my will, in a foreign country (that seemed more and more foreign by the minute) by a drug cartel that was threatening my life. I had no question whatsoever, as I listened to the man on the other end of the line, that they would do exactly what they said.

This emotional bullying continued for about fifteen minutes, when all at once the voice on the other end of the line said, "Un momento." Almost immediately another man came on the line and began the same process as the first—threatening to kill me, threatening to cut off my hands and my ears. Threatening methods of torture only a depraved lunatic could envision. Though this man was threatening me with the same things the first man had, there was something different. This man—if it is even possible—was more evil than the first.

And so it went when the third man came on the line—uglier, more sinister, more threatening, and more intense than the man before. The threats got more and more pointed. The intimidation factor went up and up and up until I was adrift in a desperate sea of fear, just trying to keep my head above water. I knew if I let down for an instant, I would be consumed by this fear and that would be the end of me.

Somehow, intuitively, I knew if I didn't keep control of my emotions, I would die. I was fighting for my life with members of this cartel, but the real fight was within my own soul. I had to keep control of myself at the exact same time these evil men were doing everything in their power to strip me of any control.

It was right in the middle of this giant battle of emotions that I heard number three say, "Un momento," or just a second. In just a very short time, I had come to hate that phrase. The intimidation and mind control practiced by these thugs was obviously carefully orchestrated. And it was incredibly effective. You start small (which actually seemed huge to me) and then ratchet it up and up and up.

The next voice on the phone announced himself as "*el jefe de todos.*" The big boss. As brutal and venomous as the other three men had been, they didn't compare in the slightest with the big boss. He spoke with the voice of a thousand raging demons, spewing hate and vileness, and weaving a disgusting tapestry of profanity and vulgar expressions as he turned the full fury of hell itself loose on me.

I have never been in the presence of anything approaching the depravity of this man. I can't imagine that standing in the presence of the prince of darkness himself could be any more intimidating, any more withering, than being in the verbal presence of this man. And even as I call him a man, I can't really imagine an actual human-being doing, saying, or being anything like this person was.

And though the threats from his predecessors had pierced my heart with terror, there was something different about the threats that came from this minion of Lucifer. When the first three said they were going to kill me, torture me, dismember me, I believed it—with all my heart. When he said those things, I could almost see a movie of those unspeakable, unthinkable things playing across the screen of my mind.

And he was the first to point out that it wasn't just my life that was in danger. He painted a profanity-laden verbal picture of what he would do to my wife and children. And it wasn't just some peaceful, die-in-your-sleep kind of killing. He droned on and on about how each would be tortured, how they would be raped, and about what a very slow and ever-so-painful death it would be. I could see in my mind's eye how sick people like this man would make their victims beg to be killed long before they actually died. No matter what I had to do, that could never be the end for my loved ones. But what control did I have?

I knew the drug cartels sponsored gangs in the States. I knew that gang members from various parts of the States could be at my house before the sun came up. Panic washed over me in wave after wave, a tsunami of fear tumbling me mercilessly for the lifetime that the big boss talked to me on the phone. There is one level of fear when you fear for yourself and for what might happen to you. There is another level of fear, infinitely more profound and more real, when those you love are being threatened by a source over which you have absolutely no control.

The fear grew inside me like a giant wolf, devouring any sense of sanity I had left. It was as if I were having an out-of-body experience. I felt like I was floating up to the ceiling, looking down at my pitiful figure lying there on the floor, and wondering how this all could have happened.

What I really wanted to do was end the pain. I wanted nothing more than to just hang up the phone, walk out the door, and breathe the night air. But I knew with an unwavering certainty that the minute I cut the connection, the men waiting outside my room would burst in and the horror these animals had been promising me would become reality. That was a chance I couldn't take. For the time being, the only safety I had was to do everything in my power to keep my wits about me and to follow their instructions to the letter.

I began to contemplate the very real possibility that I might not ever see my wife again in this life. I might never be able to hold her and comfort her. We might never be able to laugh together again. We might never again stand side by side and watch our children and grandchildren grow up with that outpouring of love and gratitude.

I might never see my children again in this life. I wouldn't be there when my youngest got married, or when my children had more children of their own, or when they had all those milestones fathers are supposed to be there for. I might never watch my grandchildren play a simple basketball game, or get married, or anything else.

But worst of all, I started thinking about the last time I'd seen each of them. Had I said everything I would have wanted to say if I was never going to see them again? My mind happened upon the Garth Brooks song "If Tomorrow Never Comes." You know the song. I paraphrased it in my mind. If tomorrow never comes, would they know how much I loved them? Did I try in every way to show them every day just how important they were to me? A prayer sprung up in my heart that they would know.

Just when I thought I had no choice but to abandon myself to the darkness without and rapidly spreading within, the big boss said, "Un momento." Of course, I couldn't help but wonder if there was something even worse coming. Panic rose from my chest into my throat, until the voice of my original captor came back on the phone.

"What's wrong with you?" he asked. "You don't need to be afraid. If you do everything we say, nothing is going to happen to you or your family." He was lifting me up, but not out of pity. He was lifting me up so that I might have a small ray of hope, which he immediately dashed by saying how he was going to cut off my feet.

In all, I talked to all four of the men several times over the next three hours. Three of them lifting me up just so they could slam me down, and the big boss doing everything within his power to drag me into the deepest, darkest recesses of hell—a place he was only too familiar with.

The onslaught was unbelievable. The intensity of their attack on me and on my psyche was immeasurable. It was relentless. There was no time whatsoever to take a breath to gain strength for the next round. Nothing. It was a powerful, relentless, unceasing pounding. I had been near my breaking point when the first man told me I had been kidnapped. I thought at that point there was no way I could go on. But I had gone on. Far beyond what I would have ever considered my limit.

I was on the roller coaster of desperation. The coaster would climb up to just where I could see there actually was light, and almost immediately it would plunge back down into the depths of hell. Each trip up toward the light went a little less high, and each trip down into hell went a little deeper into the darkness. This was a ride no one should ever have to take. But I was on it, and there was no way to get off.

Just when I thought it couldn't possibly get any worse, my original captor told me, "You need to prepare yourself. We're taking you out of the hotel and moving you to another place."

CHAPTER FIVE

THE MOVE

MIDNIGHT
THURSDAY EVENING
WYNDHAM HOTEL
CHIHUAHUA, MEXICO

THE THOUGHT THAT I WAS BEING MOVED FROM THE HOTEL loosed a shaft of fear into the center of my being. These men had been terrorizing me for three hours, and the level of fear and anxiety I had been experiencing was incalculable. I would have never believed it possible for it to go even higher. But the idea of a move brought my whole emotional state to a level of panic I could never have imagined.

My heart was pounding as I considered the implications of moving. Any hope of someone finding me was dashed. I would simply disappear, never to be heard from again. My mouth, which had been dry since the beginning, was now so dry my tongue was actually sticking to the roof of my mouth. My throat was closing down to the point I could barely breathe. I wondered how long my sweaty hands could hold the phone. The tingling in my hands and feet that had been more of an annoyance than anything up to this point was now spreading. It was like every inch of my skin was being stuck with pins and needles.

When you're being threatened, you fear the unknown. Your fear is based in what might happen. Not now, but sometime in the future. That fear is real, and it's powerful. But the declaration that I was being moved changed everything. Now it wasn't "I could be killed at some time in the future." It was "They are taking me to kill me right now." The immediacy of the whole situation—the fact that I was potentially on my way to be killed right now—pushed me almost beyond the breaking point.

Cautiously, I asked, "Where are you taking me?" They wouldn't say. I was told only that I needed to follow their instructions or I would be killed. My eyes darted around the room like a mouse trapped in a corner by the cat who is relentlessly closing in. If they wouldn't say, it must be something so distasteful even these hardened criminals couldn't talk about it.

I had a picture in my mind of a prisoner of war being hauled from one disgusting set of circumstances to another with no control and no way out. I could picture my own demise coming one small infliction at a time over the course of days or weeks.

The panic I felt was rapidly growing in strength and intensity—almost to the point I couldn't breathe. But somewhere, from deep inside, other feelings were crowding their way in as well. They were feelings I'd felt growing inside me since the house phone in the hotel first rang but which I hadn't taken the luxury of exploring or even entertaining. Still, here they were, boiling over like an angry pot of water that's been forgotten and left on too high a flame.

They were feelings of anger and bitterness. Maybe that's normal. I'm not sure. But the strange thing is, I wasn't just angry at these men. The truth is, I was surprisingly angry, frustrated, and bitter with myself.

I couldn't deny I'd had several warnings regarding the dangers in Mexico. When the grower had come to Utah to meet with us, Shawn had expressed his concerns about travel in Mexico in no uncertain terms. Our partner in McAllen, down on the Rio Grande, who hadn't been to Mexico in years, had tried to warn me of the danger as well. When Shawn and I had been in Mexico City a few months before to attend some business meetings, we had hired a car and driver from a reputable company to take us wherever we needed to go. And we did all that because of the danger.

To look at this whole situation another way, there wasn't anyone who'd thought it was wise for me to go to Mexico except the grower. And as good a man as he was, the fact that he was living in the culture made it impossible for him to see the situation the same way someone on the outside would.

No, I thought, bad things were what happened to other people in foreign countries. I had always prided myself on being able to resolve difficult situations. From the time I was a little boy, I was persuasive. I learned at an early age that if you could make a good argument for why you should be allowed to do something, you got much further than you did with whining and crying.

My service as a missionary for the church helped me to feel more comfortable talking to strangers and explaining things in an easy-to-understand and persuasive way. And that experience has served me well in my career.

Much of my career has been spent negotiating different types of deals, and I have a talent for such things. I had watched my stepfather, who worked in the potato business, create a happy, successful life, and I thought, *That's a life that would really suit me.* And so it was. My first job out of college was in a carrot operation. I was hired to be the assistant plant manager.

My first day on the job, my boss called me in.

"I have some good news and some bad news," he said. "The bad news is the plant manager quit on Friday. The good news is you're the new plant manager." So at twenty-four years old, in my first real job, I took on more responsibility than I ever had. I learned quickly that fear is not how you get things done in business. You have to convince those who work for you to do the things that need to be done. If you do it right, it builds goodwill, loyalty, and a positive attitude in the business. If you do it wrong . . .

Motivating employees gave me an opportunity to hone skills I'd started to learn on my mission. It was no different, really. As time went on and my career advanced, I realized I really like that part of my job. I have built a successful career around my ability to negotiate. So I was confident that if I got in a bind, I could talk my way out of it. That's been the story of my life.

And it's not like I was going to China, where I would be a fish out of water. I have been to Mexico and other parts of Latin America more times than I can count. I'm very fluent in the language. I understand the culture implicitly. It wouldn't be a stretch to say I'm as comfortable in Latin America as I am at home in the States. I was confident when I boarded the plane for Chihuahua that bad things happened to other people, not to me. Because of my ability to speak and negotiate, I was somehow immune from those things happening to me.

But at that moment, sitting on the end of the bed in a lonely hotel room so very far from home, I couldn't help but admit it was pride that had allowed me (or maybe even driven me) to travel to Mexico against the best wishes of people who, perhaps, had a more realistic view of the dangers than I did. Anger, frustration, and bitterness continued rising up in my throat, threatening to choke me.

For the last several seconds (or had it been hours or days?) I had allowed myself to descend into the deepest, darkest depths of despair. My pride had brought me to this point, and in the next few minutes—not likely more than that—it was going to cost me my life. The fear of never seeing my family again on this earth forced its way to the front of my mind. They might never know what even happened to me. People disappear without a trace in Mexico. I knew that. It was looking like there was a very real possibility I would become one of them. I had been doing my best to keep my head above water emotionally, but now I was losing that battle. I was sliding into a place that was so lonely, so sad, and so senseless I could no longer cope.

And suddenly, just as I was about to abandon myself to this powerful, primal despair, I sensed a warmth, as if angels were lifting me out of this abyss I had allowed myself to sink into. A voice I recognized immediately as the Holy Spirit fairly screamed at me, "This isn't over yet. You don't give up until it's over. You don't ever quit. You get in there and fight until your very last breath." I realized that was right. As long as I kept my wits about me, I still had a chance. A small chance, to be sure, but a chance.

A question began to form in my mind as I rose out of the gloom: "Why are they holding me?" When they first called, they said there was a "war" between cartels in the hotel. Then they told me I was their captive. But why? Why me? Why here? Why now? And so, feeling I really had nothing to lose at this point, I decided to ask.

Being emboldened by an internal voice my mother had taught me at an early age to always trust, I asked, "Why are you holding me?" knowing as a negotiator that until I understood their position, I would never be able to negotiate a positive outcome.

"You were just in the wrong place at the wrong time," my captor responded coldly.

"What do you want from me?" I asked.

"We want you to do as you're told," was his terse reply.

Going through this line of questioning was more than just a negotiation. I was buying time as my mind raced. *I can't leave this hotel,* I thought. *My only hope of rescue is to stay here.*

There was a credit card record that I had been there. There were phone records. My grower knew he had picked me up there and dropped me off there. This hotel was the only connection I had with the outside world. If I went anywhere else, there would be no record, no nothing. I would simply vanish into thin air.

"There's no reason to move me," I told my captor. "Just let me stay here. I'm happy to do whatever you want. Just don't move me."

Although this room was the scene of my night of terror, it was a known quantity. And there was at least a small (some would say microscopic) glimmer of hope that someone might find me here when I didn't catch my plane in the morning. What was outside this hotel, I could only imagine. And I couldn't foresee a single scenario where leaving would be better than staying—not one.

For the next hour, we talked. I was desperately trying to get information, and my captor was giving me nothing. I tried to get him to reconsider his plan to move me, but he was having none of it. For all my skill in conflict resolution, I was accomplishing nothing.

"It's not your choice whether you stay or go. You're leaving, and that's that." He said it with some finality. "Listen carefully. If you don't follow these instructions perfectly, you're dead."

He went over the instructions again and again. I was to leave everything in the hotel. I was to take nothing but my cell phone and my charger. No other devices, no suitcases, no toiletries, nothing. Absolutely nothing but my phone and charger. He had me write down the address of where I was going—another hotel. I wrote it in my planner.

"When I tell you, you're going to walk down the hall to the lobby. We will be watching you the whole way. You won't see us, but we'll be there. You'll walk across the lobby and out the front door. You will talk to nobody on your way out. Once in the street, you'll hail a taxi and give him the address of the hotel you just wrote down. You'll check in at the hotel in the name of Manuel Orozco. You will leave the cell phone on speaker the entire way. If you cut the line, we will move in and kill you. Remember, we are watching you every step of the way."

I could see what they were doing. By having me check in under a Mexican name, even if someone found the hotel I was going to, if they looked at the register searching for an American, there would be nothing there to indicate an American was even staying there. I felt like my captors had just pounded the last nail in my coffin. Of course, if someone saw me, they would know I was an American. But nobody would see me. It was the middle of the night. There would be no one there to witness me checking in. After I checked in, I would be locked in my room and nobody would know there was an American in the hotel.

He then had me repeat the whole thing to him. Then he repeated it back to me again, and so on, four or five more times.

While we were going through all this, the thought kept coming to me, *I've got to leave a trail for someone to follow if they come looking for me. But how?*

I decided if someone came looking for me, they would be most concerned if the room looked like it had been ransacked. I knew there was a possibility the cartel would come along behind me and "sanitize" everything so nobody would have any indication I had ever been there. I also knew if what I did was too obvious, it could cost me my life.

But ransacking the room seemed the best idea. If nobody from the cartel came, it would be an alert to someone looking for me. If they did follow up, I could simply tell them that's the way I live—that I'm a messy person by nature.

I felt like it would work, so as I repeated the instructions of my captor, I went around the room making it look as ransacked as I thought I could explain if I had to.

Finally, the voice on the other end of the line said, "It's time to move. Get your phone and your charger and walk out the door." I had started out the door when he said, "There are three men in the lobby. Those are our men. Say nothing to them. Don't even look at them. Just walk through the lobby and out the front door."

The fear that had first gripped me when they told me I was being moved returned with vengeance. I walked down the hall to the lobby on shaky knees. When I saw the three men in the lobby, my fear spiked to a level I didn't know was possible. *Would these three men be my killers? Would they make it quick and painless, or would they draw it out over a period of days or even weeks? Would I die with some sort of dignity, or would I go out screaming like a little girl?* Those thoughts and a thousand more flooded my consciousness to the point I could hardly walk.

Out the front door and into the night air I went. I looked up and down the street for more cartel members. I didn't see anyone, but they told me that although I wouldn't see them, they were there.

The night was crisp and cool. It felt good to fill my lungs with something other than the stale air of my hotel room. I couldn't help but wonder how many more nights of breathing clean, crisp air I would have. I knew I'd better savor it. This might be the last one.

The street wasn't well lit, by any means, but it wasn't dark, either. There was one streetlight in the middle of a long block, casting foreboding shadows on the buildings. I looked both up and down the street for a taxi. There was nothing. It was about one o'clock in the morning, and this wasn't a particularly busy street. What could I do but wait?

"Hurry up," my captor said, his threatening, guttural voice intruding into my thoughts and fears. "What are you waiting for?"

"There are no taxis," I replied.

"Find one," he said impatiently.

"I'm not from here. I have no idea where to find one," I said.

With that, I started to pace up and down the street. Occasionally I would see a car coming. I wondered if it was a taxi. Or maybe it was the cartel preparing a drive-by shooting. I was so completely frazzled I knew I wasn't thinking clearly or even logically. I was just going through the motions.

Each car that passed me brought both hope and fear. On the one hand I hoped a taxi would come before my captor got frustrated and told the three men inside to just come kill me. On the other hand, I hoped a taxi would never come and that my captor would tell me to go back into the hotel and up to my room.

I wasn't sure exactly what I wanted. Right then, I just wanted this whole nightmare to be over.

CHAPTER SIX

INTO THE NIGHT

1:30 A.M.
FRIDAY MORNING
OUTSIDE THE WYNDHAM HOTEL
CHIHUAHUA, MEXICO

THE RUMBLING TIRES OF EACH CAR THAT PASSED catapulted my anxiety to new heights. In my room, it had been just me. My tormentors, although in the room via telephone, weren't right there with me. Being alone was difficult. But being out in the open and totally exposed was more unnerving, if that's even possible. I didn't know what the cartel intended to do with me at this point. Was I to be an example to other business people who might be considering doing business in Mexico? Were they going to do some horrific thing to me as retribution for governmental policies on both sides of the border? Would it be a semipublic execution with video all over the internet, or would I just quietly disappear?

The thought that I might be being held for ransom never found a serious place in my mind. It passed through a time or two, but the way I was being treated didn't feel like any hostage-for-ransom situation I'd ever seen on television. And, after all, that's the only experience I'd had with kidnappers. I'd never been kidnapped, and I didn't know anyone who had. In fact, I didn't know anyone who knew someone who'd been kidnapped. My only experience with kidnapping was television, and this didn't fit the stereotype.

So, once again, I was swimming upstream in a river of uncertainty. Every time I tried to force things to make sense, they just wouldn't. And I suppose my captors liked it that way. It was like I was trying to balance on top of a slightly underinflated ball. Reality was constantly shifting under my feet as I struggled and struggled to stay upright. It was constant, relentless, unchanging. And, truthfully, it was wearing me down and wearing me out physically, mentally, and emotionally.

I had been pacing up and down the block for almost fifteen minutes. My captor had been talking to me almost nonstop since I'd exited the hotel. He was becoming increasingly frustrated and angry. I was becoming less and less optimistic and more and more fearful of my ultimate outcome.

Suddenly, I realized I'd left my day planner in my room. And not only had I left it behind, I'd left it open to the page where I'd written the address of the new hotel. My first thought was, *I've got to go back up to my room and get my planner.* But returning to the room was not in the instructions I'd received. And the thought of running the gauntlet of those three men in the lobby was also not something I had any desire to do.

I realized as I thought about it for a few minutes that I had been instructed to write down the address. So I'd followed that instruction. Second, I had been instructed to take nothing but my phone and charger. I'd also followed that instruction. Finally, I knew that if the police came to that room looking for me before the cartel cleaned it out, the book would provide a clue as to where I'd gone.

I decided to leave the book in the room and hope for the best.

Just then, a taxi came around the corner and into view. I raised my hand in the international symbol of needing a ride. He pulled to the curb, and I got in. I searched his face for some clue as to whether he was complicit with the cartel, but the dim light of the car's interior didn't give me any clues. I had repeated the address of the new hotel to my captors enough times that it was engraved in my memory. I gave the taxi driver the address. He nodded that he knew it, and we started off down the street.

A million thoughts flooded my mind. If this man wasn't part of the whole thing, all I had to do was put my phone on mute, explain that I was being kidnapped, and have him take me to the police station, where I could get help. On the other hand, if he was complicit and I made that request, I might end up out in the country with a bullet in the back of my head. This taxi driver really didn't seem like he was part of everything, but I couldn't be sure—and certainly not sure enough to bet my life on it. That's the choice I had to make in the moment. Was I confident enough that this man was not part of the cartel that I would put my very life on the table like so many chips in a blackjack game? The answer was no. Definitely no.

As we rode along in silence, I wrestled with the concept of taking the driver into my confidence. But it just didn't feel right. He hadn't been waiting there in front of the hotel when I came out the front door, but he apparently hadn't driven up to the hotel randomly. There had certainly been time for the cartel to call him and have him come get me, and it was very possible he was one of them. There was nothing in the situation to give me confidence, so I just sat in silence.

I've had many people say, "Oh, you should have done this or you should have done that." Yes, in retrospect, maybe I should have. And if I could have removed all the anxiety, all the insecurity, all the stress, and been able to make a completely dispassionate, reasoned judgment, I might well have done many things differently. But when your life is on the line—and I don't mean just your livelihood or your relationships or whatever. I mean your life—you don't think clearly. You don't think dispassionately. You don't make reasoned judgments.

I don't care how analytical you are, how in control of your emotions you are, how experienced you are; when your life is truly in danger, all of that goes out the window. What you're left with is pure fight or flight. The sympathetic nervous system kicks in, and everything you thought you knew is gone. It's not logical. It's not methodical. It's not even something you handle consciously. It's just you and all the adrenaline your body can produce.

And it's not just that way emotionally. It's also that way spiritually. A saying in World War II was "There are no atheists in foxholes." When you're that completely isolated, that terrified, that emotionally drained, that alone, you have nowhere else to turn but to God. Even those for whom God has had no meaning find themselves feeling after Him.

I had been praying through the whole ordeal, but as the situation escalated and the outlook grew increasingly dire, the intensity of my prayers increased accordingly. As I rode along those nearly deserted streets in the middle of the night with a man who might well be my executioner, I begged God to give me strength. I asked for guidance and protection. I pleaded for help from above.

And so it went until we arrived at the new hotel. The taxi driver never spoke to me, and other than giving him the address, I never spoke to him. It was only ten minutes or so to the new hotel. My original hotel had been in a quiet part of town, and this one was even quieter.

At the curb, I paid the taxi driver with some loose change from my pocket and said goodbye. As I handed him the money, I once again looked deep into his eyes, searching for some clue whether he was an active participant in my nightmare or just an unwitting bystander, dragged in through no fault of his own—a person in the wrong place at the wrong time. There was no clue whatsoever in his face, which was odd. I can usually read people pretty well. But this man could have been at the poker tables in Vegas. His face didn't reveal any trace of whether or not he was one of them.

The hotel was a nondescript, garden-variety, mom-and-pop Mexican hotel. There was nothing noteworthy about it, really. There wasn't much of a lobby but, rather, just a check-in area. I walked up to the desk, where the receptionist was waiting for me.

I don't know if it was because it was late, but there was very little conversation. It was all business. She gathered the usual information and entered it into the computer. When asked my name, I hesitated, just an instant. I had been told what name to use. It was a Mexican name.

But just as I was about to give her the Mexican name, a voice inside my head screamed, "Don't use the Mexican name! Give a name that will be recognizable to friends and family (or to the FBI) should they make it this far looking for me." But what name could I use? I couldn't use the name of my son, because the last name would give it away. I couldn't use the name of one of my sons-in-law because they were young and it would put their lives at risk. I couldn't do that to my daughters. I decided to use the name of my stepfather. Should the cartel go looking for him, he would be hard to find. He's an older widower, and I simply felt that if I had the time to ask him if it was okay to use his name, not only would it be okay, he would insist I do so. I knew it was close enough for an investigator or a family member to find, but not close enough to cost me or my stepfather our lives.

She looked at me, expecting an answer, and I said, "My name is Kenneth Shepherd." She entered the name without flinching. I knew in the instant I gave her an Anglo name there might be hell to pay later from the cartel—they were listening to the whole thing on the speaker phone—but I also knew that without that, it would be impossible for anyone to figure out what had happened to me.

Once she had entered all the information, she asked how I was going to pay for the room. My captor had instructed me to pay with cash (obviously to avoid being able to track the transaction), but I had told him I didn't have that much cash. That wasn't exactly true, of course. I had cash, but I knew if I paid in cash there would be no record of my whereabouts. He was not happy, but what could he do? I pulled out my credit card and handed it to the receptionist. She ran it through the machine without any apparent recognition that the name on the card didn't match the name on the room.

One thing I knew for sure was the credit card transaction would lead investigators to this hotel. The second thing I knew was the name Kenneth Shepherd would be recognizable to anyone in my family. I was still on the radar. As much as the cartel members had tried to make it otherwise, I had yet to disappear. I knew as long as my movements were still visible to the outside world, I had a glimmer of hope.

I also found it interesting that she never asked for my papers. I've never checked into a hotel in a foreign country where they didn't ask to take a copy of my passport. It seemed odd to me that she didn't ask for anything, but at this point I was so fatigued I just wrote it off to the lateness of the hour. Maybe she didn't ask because she was instructed not to. Maybe it was an oversight. I will never know. But there's no question it added to my already overwhelming uncertainty about everything that was happening.

We got the registration done, she gave me a key, and I went up to the room.

Approaching the door to the room, I had a sick feeling in the pit of my stomach. As I reached out to put the key in the lock, I wondered what—or who—awaited me on the other side of the door. Had they brought me here to kill me? Was this the end of the road? Why wouldn't they take me out in the desert and kill me? Maybe they wanted it to be more public. Maybe, maybe, maybe, maybe . . . The only way to find out was put the key in the door, turn the knob, and go in.

The room was small and not particularly well-appointed. It reminded me of a Super 8 motel of twenty years ago in the States. It was clean and tidy. And, best of all, there was nobody waiting for me on the other side of the door.

Absentmindedly, I walked over to the window and looked out. I expected to see people looking up at my window. Cartel members just waiting for some excuse to finish this once and for all. What I saw was a quiet little street with nobody about. I closed the curtain and walked over and sat on the foot of the bed.

Just as I sat down, the phone erupted with a string of profanity and angry expressions all pointed at me. I had almost forgotten my captor had been on the line through all of this. "Why did you not use the name we told you to use?" He stammered, almost apoplectic.

I knew he would be angry, but I was pretty much to the point where I felt like saying, "Look. If you're going to kill me, then do it. But quit talking about it." What I said was something much different.

"The fact is, I forgot the name. I tried and tried to remember, but I couldn't do it. My mind isn't working very well. In the stress of the situation, I forgot the name, so I used the name Kenneth Shepherd. I know you told me to use the Latin name, but at least I followed the cardinal rule: I didn't divulge my own name." I guess I must have sounded convincing, because he bought it.

"Who is Kenneth Shepherd?" he asked.

"Nobody," I replied. "Kenneth is my favorite name. If I could have named myself, I would have named myself Kenneth. As far as Shepherd, that refers to the good shepherd—the Man Upstairs. I figured if I ever needed help and blessings from the Man Upstairs, this was it. So that was the last name I chose."

Although he was still very angry, he bought the story. I had a strange sense of relief that this hadn't gone any worse than it had.

As I sat there on the bed, exhaustion started to overtake me. I'm not a night person in the first place, and after mega-dosing on adrenaline for four hours, I felt like I used to feel when I got home on a Saturday night after fixing the fence on the neighbor's ranch in the mountains of Colorado. As a very young teenager, I would work from before sunup to well after sundown six days a week on the mountain. By the time I got home on Saturday night, I wasn't just tired. I was exhausted to the center of my bones.

You can only stay amped up to the degree I had been for so long, then you have to come down. It's impossible for your mind and body to sustain such wild swings of emotional ups and downs for that long—nonstop—without something giving. I knew I had to be sharp to stay alive. But I wasn't sharp. And, worse, there was no more reserve to draw on. I was spent.

I lay back on the bed, looking for some relief while a profound sense of melancholy began to overtake me. I was sinking into a place I had been fighting for three hours to stay out of. But now there was no fight left in me. I sank deeper and deeper as the turbid waters of complete and utter despair closed in over my head.

CHAPTER SEVEN

PROFOUND DARKNESS

2:30 A.M.
FRIDAY MORNING
FIESTA INN HOTEL
CHIHUAHUA, MEXICO

I SUPPOSE THE THING THAT REALLY BROUGHT ME to the point of exhaustion was the change in my captors' tactics. For the first three to four hours they had been in my ear constantly, tag-teaming me, berating me, threatening me, and keeping me at such a fever pitch emotionally that I could just barely function.

There had been four of them taking turns. Relentlessly wearing me down. And the truth is, they had been incredibly effective. But suddenly I realized that had changed. From thirty minutes or so before I left the first hotel, I had only been talking to my original captor. The others had gone. And while I was in that original room, he had been talking constantly.

But there had been little communication as I left the hotel and rode over in the taxi. Since arriving in the new hotel room, there were lapses in our conversation of three to four minutes.

At first I welcomed these moments of silence. After very literally having the devil in my ear nonstop for nearly four hours, it was a relief to have a minute or two to myself.

There were only two downsides to the silence. First, although the voice of evil would leave me to myself for a few minutes, there was never any question it would be back. In many ways, the anticipation was as bad or worse than the actual voice. The break was welcome, but knowing he would soon be back made it so I really couldn't catch my breath.

The second downside was even worse. While I had been engaged in the conversation from the beginning, I didn't really have time to process what was going on. For the next forty-five minutes, I would have many of those little interludes to process my thoughts. And that wasn't good. As I analyzed the whole experience from the beginning, I realized that in spite of the optimism I had forced myself to maintain, it was increasingly obvious I was never going home to my family.

I slipped deeper and deeper into despair. Down and down I went, wondering if I would ever reach the bottom. As time passed and my thoughts grew darker and darker, the hopelessness of my situation surrounded me like an impenetrable wall. No matter which way I turned, there was no hope—none.

I had had a prayer in my heart all night. Since arriving at this new hotel, I had started to cry unto the Lord in what can only be described as mighty prayer. I'd read that term in the scriptures before, but until that moment, I really didn't know what it meant. I poured out my soul to God with an intensity I had never used before. I knew I was powerless to do anything for myself. I also knew the only hope I had was for God to intervene in my behalf. That was the object and desire of these intense prayers. But even as I prayed, I could feel the powers of darkness overtaking me.

It was at this point my past, present, and future collided. The room started to gather darkness. The lights were on, but I was surrounded by a darkness and a dampness—a powerful evil—that began to penetrate my very soul. I have never before or since felt anything like it. It was terrifying. It was the very power of Lucifer himself arrayed in all his might and majesty. It literally took my breath away.

For the first time, I became aware of the presence of evil spirits in the room with me. Demons raging against the light—raging against all that was good, all that was holy. And, most importantly, they were raging for my soul. I was in a battle for my very existence. I could feel them gaining strength.

Their epithets penetrated my consciousness like a dagger. "You're no good! You're going to die tonight, and you're going to spend eternity with us. Whatever good you've done in your life is nothing in comparison to the mistakes you've made. You will never be forgiven. You will never see your family again—not in this life or the next. You are a horrible person. Get ready to die. Tonight will be the end of you forever."

The voices weren't something I could hear with my ears, but they were audible to my soul. And not just audible. I could *feel* their taunting. Like the shockwave from a huge explosion, they shook me to the core, pinning me to the bed. The room was well lit and perfectly quiet. But I could nonetheless hear those voices raging around me, and I could literally feel their presence as they brushed up against me. They were circling like wolves moving in for the kill, saliva dripping from their teeth, the taste of blood driving them out of their minds.

The room was closing in on me. Intellectually, I knew it was a good-sized room, but it was getting smaller by the minute. And not just that. The brightly colored bedspread was fading before my eyes to more muted tones. Sounds of the street outside, which at first were barely audible, were taking on a sharper or "tinny" sound. When I had entered the room, it smelled clean and fresh. Now it was taking on an older, more tired aroma. The stress and the late hour were combining to change my perception of reality. It was surreal.

In that moment, in those circumstances, I was afraid of dying, mostly because I wondered—maybe even doubted—if all the good I'd done in my life would be enough. I was afraid of what the next several hours or days might entail, wondering what unspeakable things they would do to me before taking my life. I couldn't even bear to consider the thought of not seeing my family again. It was an unmeasurable weight, crushing me, pushing me down into the depths of the abyss.

I felt without any question my death was imminent.

I was very literally paralyzed with fear. I couldn't make my body move. And even as I say that, those words don't convey in the slightest what I was feeling. I wondered if my heart would stop. It was all I could do to summon one more breath. I was literally frozen—unable to move.

Just as I was about to abandon myself to the darkness, something miraculous happened. In the very moment I was about to be completely destroyed by the evil surrounding me, a thought forced its way through the dark cocoon that encased me like some sort of spiritual coffin and slashed through my despair as it penetrated my mind.

It was the teachings of my mother. For just one moment in time, I was transported to the kitchen table in the house I grew up in. Seated around that table were my siblings, my mother, and me. My mother was a master teacher and gifted storyteller. In that moment, I was once again listening as she told the story of Daniel from the Bible. Daniel refuses to cease praying to his God and is thrown in prison. Even there he follows the word of God and is cast into the lion's den. Because of his faith, those hungry lions, which were prowling around him, intent on eating him, suddenly lay down and went to sleep.

I could hear her voice as clearly in that hotel room as I heard it so many times around that kitchen table. "Evil has no power over you that you can't resist. No matter how powerful evil spirits may seem, they are always subject to the faith of righteous men." Instead of pleading to God to spare my life, my prayers turned to casting away these evil spirits. With all the faith I could muster, I stood, raised my arm to the square, and prayed that God would banish these demons from my presence.

That's exactly what happened. They had gathered one here and one there until I was overwhelmed by them. But when they left, it was so sudden it startled me and opened the door for something incredible to happen.

As quickly as the evil spirits departed, taking with them the darkness and the gloom, I felt the room and my soul filling with light. And I had an experience I'd never had before. I felt the presence in the room of specific people who had passed on. I felt my dear mother. It was almost as if she wrapped her arms around me and ran her fingers through my hair like she did when I was a little boy. I felt her communicate to me that everything would be fine. Not that I would be spared, but that things would be fine.

I felt the presence of a little grandson who had passed in a late-term miscarriage only a week before. I felt my grandfather, who had always watched over me when I was young. And also a close friend who had been taken in a motorcycle accident earlier that year.

I didn't talk to these departed loved ones. I didn't ask any questions. I simply felt their presence and their love and the strength they were sent to give me. We didn't need words to communicate. The message they were sent to give was delivered in a very powerful way—a way that words never could. How did it happen? I don't know. But I know it was real. It was unmistakable. And I drew strength from it.

Throughout my life I had had many experiences with divine guidance. I had felt the presence of what I would have called angels in the past, meaning I had felt I was surrounded by "good." I recalled a time out in the mountains with friends on our motorcycles. I somehow found myself separated from the group, but I wasn't concerned. I thought I knew the way back to camp. I dropped into a drainage, over the next ridge, and down into a canyon, only to realize I was lost. I shut off my bike to see if I could hear those of my friends. There was no sound.

Like I had always done when I was in a bind, I sought divine guidance. I had no idea where I was, but I knew God knew where I was and the best way back to camp. I offered a sincere prayer with faith that God would guide me back to my friends. And as had happened in the past, I felt the presence of the Holy Spirit as he gave me step-by-step directions back to camp. You have those experiences as you need them and as you seek them, and sometimes you forget how miraculous they really are.

But this was different. While it was not uncommon for me to receive the guidance, help, and comfort of the Holy Spirit, I had never felt the presence of someone I knew specifically. I felt like God had sent very specific, very carefully chosen spirits to me in my extremity to comfort and strengthen me at a time when I had drained the last drop of my reserves. That experience didn't last very long. A few minutes at most. But it gave me the strength to keep moving forward.

All I know for sure, after passing through that trying time in my life, is that evil is real—as real and as tangible as anything there is. And that goodness and love are real—as real and as tangible as anything there is. From the time Adam walked out of the garden and into the world we now call home, the battle between good and evil has been waged and will continue to be waged until the end.

The blessing for me was this: my brief encounter with the love and kindness and goodness of these departed loved ones strengthened me. I still felt in my heart of hearts like I would probably lose my life before this was all over, but I felt peace. I felt strength. I felt like I would be "fine," whatever that meant, just like my mother had communicated to me.

CHAPTER EIGHT

PEACE

3:00 A.M.
FRIDAY MORNING
FIESTA INN HOTEL
CHIHUAHUA, MEXICO

BY THIS TIME, IT WAS 3:00 A.M. As I contemplated what had just happened, my heart overflowed with gratitude. I had been in the deepest, darkest recesses of hell and had been tormented by multitudes of demons bent on my destruction. I had been delivered into the light and into the spiritual presence of those who had passed on before and who obviously had the assignment to care for and watch over me.

I have heard people say that the veil between this life and the next is very thin. Until this moment, I don't think I realized what that meant. But the veil had been thin, and it still was. My heart was filled with love for those closest to me, those on the earth and those who had passed on to the next life. But most of all, I was deeply, profoundly grateful for having been delivered from the awful gloom and despair of hell itself.

But delivered unto what? I was sure my death was imminent. I felt certain I would be dead before the sun came up. It wasn't a panicky feeling like it had been. It wasn't a feeling of desperation or despair. It just was.

As I pondered my situation, thoughts of my family overwhelmed me. I wasn't afraid to die. I had been close enough to the other side of the veil already tonight that I really held no fear of dying. I was, however, very concerned for my family. I was sad about not being there for the special events in the lives of my children and grandchildren. I was sad about not being there to protect and defend them throughout their lives. But I wasn't afraid to die.

As I went deeper and deeper into my thoughts, I felt an intense need to say something to the loved ones I would leave behind. But how? I had been threatened with my life if I tried to make contact of any kind. Those weren't idle threats. There was no doubt in my mind whatsoever that they would act on those threats.

I thought about writing a letter, but how would I ever be able to send it? I thought about leaving it in the room, but I knew when they came to clean the room it would be destroyed. I thought about texting, but they said my devices were all bugged and it would never get out.

The peace I had begun to feel was dissipating rapidly. Thoughts of my mother and my siblings once again flooded my mind. "Bob? Bob get up. It's time to go outside." That was one of my mother's favorite things to do as a family. We would get up before dawn, take a blanket out into our huge grove of trees, and wait for the birds to wake up and start singing.

More than sixty years before, my great grandfather had planted what amounted to a forest on our property. We had well over one hundred quaking aspen, stately fir, and other trees that reached high into the sky. Early in the morning, just before the sun came up, if you were quiet and still, one bird would begin to sing. Soon it was joined by another. Then another and another. Before you knew it, the entire grove of trees was alive with the beautiful sound of the birds who lived there.

It was in those moments after listening and feeling the beauty of the forest that my mother would begin to teach. Sometimes she told stories from the Bible. Sometimes she opened the scriptures and shared verses with us. But that was always the pattern: stop, be still (inside and out), and enjoy. Then and only then were you ready to be taught. I think of those patterns today as I use them with my own children, and I marvel at how inspired they really are.

And at this horrible moment, for just an instant, I found myself back under those trees that surrounded our house. I could hear my mother's voice as clearly as if she were standing right next to me. "And so you can see, children, that no matter how bad things get, no matter how difficult or dangerous the path, there is always peace, direction, and comfort to be found in the scriptures."

She was right, of course. She always was. Peace and comfort do come when you read the scriptures. So I did what I always did in times like this. I opened the scriptures app on my phone and I began to read.

As I was reading, one particular verse stuck out to me, and I thought, *I need to make a note on this verse, so I don't forget.* That's when it hit me. I could make a note on my scriptures here, and it would be available on all my devices both here and at home. It was hidden in the sense that my captors would have to go all the way through my scriptures to find it, and they certainly weren't about to do that. It wasn't something that was sent electronically, so it wasn't subject to interception by the cartel. It was the perfect plan.

But where in the scriptures? As hard as it would be for the cartel to find, it would be equally hard for my family to find. They too would have to go clear through my scriptures to find what I'd written. And they wouldn't even know there was anything to be found there. Then the thought came, "Tag your favorite verse of scripture with a note. If your family looks through your scriptures, they will start with your favorite verse."

My favorite verse in all of holy writ is found in the Book of Mormon in Alma, chapter 5, verse 14: *And now behold, I ask of you, my brethren of the church, have ye spiritually been born of God? Have ye received his image in your countenances? Have ye experienced this mighty change in your hearts?* Everyone in my family knew that was my favorite scripture, and I knew if they were ever to go look through my scriptures, that's where they would most likely start.

So that's what I did. In between my captor saying, "Are you there? You're not thinking of doing anything stupid are you?" and the three to four minutes that passed before he broke the silence again, I wrote a note to my family and attached it to my favorite scripture in Alma. I could only pray that God would lead them to it at some point.

Before I write the words of that note here, I ask you this: If you only had two to three hours to live and you wanted to make a final declaration of love to those you care about, what would you say? Keep in mind, you're writing on a little keyboard on a phone. You don't have the luxury of a word processor.

I began formulating what I would say in my mind. *I'd like them to know how much I love them, first and foremost. I'd like to give them some final counsel, although right this minute, I don't know what that would be.*

Suddenly, my thoughts were interrupted.

"*Roberto, estas alli?*"

Of course I was still here. He knew that. Why did he keep saying that? Where else would I go?

"*Si.*" My answer was short, almost curt.

"*Estas dormido?*"

Like I could just lie down on the bed and sleep like a baby.

"*No. Estoy pendiente*," I said. Still with you.

"*Bueno*."

And the phone went silent once more.

I found my way to Alma in my Book of Mormon app and began to try to put my thoughts down.

I wrote:

> *Family, I love you so much. I'm not sure if I will ever see you again, but know that you have made my life so complete and full. Being a husband to the most wonderful woman in the world has been the greatest blessing of my life. We have been blessed with incredible children—all seven of them: four of my own children and three in-laws. I could not love my family any more than I do. I love that the things we have taught our kids are being lived and observed in their lives. Lincoln and Henry [grandsons] and soon to be William are the lights of our lives. Nothing better than being a grandpa. The experience I am going through right now just south of El Paso has been the most frightening experience of my life. At first, I was completely panicked and didn't know if I could get through this. But I have felt guardian angels by my side . . . Mother, Papa, Smith baby number two, and Ronnie Crowther. I have been awake all night and on the phone with those who hold me captive.*

As I read and reread those words, my heart was burdened by the fact that this might be my final communication with those I loved the most in this life, and that it might be a long time before someone stumbled upon the note. All I could do was put my faith and trust in God to lead them to it and go forward.

Because of everything I'd been through for the last several hours, I felt close to Him. I had been praying with increasing intensity, and as I did, I felt Him near me. But even as I prayed intently to God, the taunts of the demons so intent on my complete and utter destruction still crowded their way into my consciousness. "You're not good enough. You're not returning to God. You'll spend the rest of eternity here with us."

I became more and more concerned. I felt I had lived a pretty good life. I'd always tried to do what's right. But I suppose when you know your death is only minutes away, you have to ask the question: "Am I okay?" I believe even avowed atheists, if they know their death is minutes away, might wonder, "What if those religious people were right? What if there is a God?"

In my darkest moment, those demons from the infernal pit played on my insecurity. "You're not worthy. Your life wasn't good enough." And now that was exactly the question that took control of my mind. "I'm going to die very, very soon. What's to become of me for eternity?" Was my life good enough to return to live with God, or were those tortured souls from hell really right? Would I spend the rest of eternity with them?

I again turned to the scriptures for comfort. The Book of Mormon talks about men of the church who were firm, steadfast, immovable, willing, and diligent. I thought about how I had lived my life. If they ever found my body and held a funeral, would people use those adjectives to describe me? More importantly, could I, in all honesty, use those words to describe my own life? And then I realized it wasn't important what my friends or I thought. What really mattered was whether God would use those words to describe my life.

I continued reading of a different group of people. "Now they did not sin ignorantly, for they knew the will of God concerning them, therefore they did willfully rebel against God."

I started back over my life, beginning with my earliest memories of childhood and moving forward. I wasn't perfect. Nobody is. I had made mistakes—some serious. I could easily see that the times I had sinned in my life, I had done so knowing what I did was wrong but, being weak in the flesh, had done it anyway. I felt like in those times I truly had "willfully rebelled against God."

Was that my answer? As doubt and despair began once again to creep into my soul, I cast my mind back on what I had been taught about the Atonement of Jesus Christ. I thought about the many times I had heard the leaders of my church say, "The Atonement of Jesus Christ has the power to erase guilt."

One leader of my church made the following statement when he was near the end of his life: "I have considered my life and there is nothing for which I have not utilized the Atonement of Jesus Christ to repent of my sins and receive forgiveness for those things that I've done that were not correct. The atonement leaves no tracks or traces. What it cleans it cleans. What it heals it heals."

I had utilized the repentance process in my life many times to apply the Atonement of Jesus Christ. I knew my life was nowhere near as good as this great leader's, but if what he said about the Atonement healing us thoroughly and completely was true, maybe there was hope for me. I began to pray in earnest. I prayed with an intensity I had never before managed. Like a man dying of thirst in the desert needs water, I needed to know if the Atonement of Jesus Christ had really cleansed me—healed me. I desperately needed to be sure it would make up the difference at the Final Judgment. I wasn't seeking some sort of "deathbed repentance." I knew that wasn't possible. I was seeking to know from God Himself if my efforts throughout my life, combined with the Atonement of Jesus Christ, had been sufficient to allow me to return and live with Him.

After about forty-five minutes of pouring my heart out, pleading for God to let me know of my standing before Him, I got an answer. I knew that I hadn't been perfect. I knew that my mistakes were numerous—too numerous to count. But I had a powerful witness that because of my sincere effort to repent throughout my life when I made mistakes, the Atonement of Jesus Christ would make up the difference for my shortcomings at the Final Judgment.

Once I felt that everything would be "fine" with me, just like my mother had communicated, I began to pray for my family. I wanted to be sure we would see each other again, if not in this life, then in the next. It wasn't long before I felt a confirmation that we would again meet and rejoice together. In my heart, I felt certain it would be in the next life. Still, it was a tremendous relief. For the moment, in spite of everything that was happening, I was at peace.

CHAPTER NINE

THOSE WHO DESPITEFULLY USE YOU

4:00 A.M.
FRIDAY MORNING
FIESTA INN HOTEL
CHIHUAHUA, MEXICO

I GLANCED AT THE CLOCK, AND IT WAS 4:00 A.M. I had been held captive for seven grueling hours. Having been able to write down a few of my thoughts for my family had lifted part of the burden of contemplating my imminent death. Also, the witness of the Holy Spirit that the way I'd lived my life wouldn't keep me from returning to my Father in Heaven and those family members who had passed on before helped lift even more of that burden.

Finding some peace and feeling like I could almost begin to breathe again gave me a chance to really ponder death—not just "death," but my death. It's interesting to me how we take incredibly stressful concepts—like death—and view them in the abstract. For example, we talk about death in general. That doesn't create too much angst. Then we start to zoom in and talk about "my" death. That's a little more stressful. But even then, when I view my death as some event that will occur far away in a future I have no idea about, it's not terribly threatening. And yet when we zoom in closer and talk about my death that is going to occur in the next few minutes, it's incredibly stressful.

When I think about my death in the future, I don't need to worry too much about whether I'm qualified to return and live with God, or anything else, really. I will work that out sometime in the future. There's plenty of time for such things, after all. But if my death is within the next few minutes, there are things that need to be taken care of now. Immediately.

As I pondered what it might be like to cross that great divide and stand in the presence of God to be judged by Him, a scripture from the fifth chapter of Matthew flashed across the screen of my mind: "But I say unto you, love your enemies, bless them that curse you, do good to them that hate you, and pray for them which despitefully use you and persecute you."

I knew exactly why that scripture had come into my mind and who it was talking about. For the last seven hours, I had struggled with feelings I had never known. I hated these men with an intensity that frightened me. I didn't know how to deal with it. I'd never hated anyone in my life. It wasn't in my nature.

Of course, there are people I don't care for. That's true for everyone. There are people I avoid because of how they make me feel when I'm around them. There are people whose actions I find disgusting. But hate? No. I'd never hated anyone in my life. And to be completely honest, while I have always found hate to be decidedly unattractive in others, I found it even more distasteful when it was me with the problem. Hate is not a religious concept, by any means. Hate has no place in anyone's life, especially not mine.

And lest we get confused with the semantics, we should probably define what hate is and what it's not. The media and the cacophony of voices on social media would have you believe that if you disagree with someone, that's hate. And if you should be so bold as to rise up and share your opinion of something that disagrees with their view of the world, that's hate speech. No. Absolutely not.

Hate is much deeper and goes far beyond any disagreement or voicing of opinion. Hate, in its most basic, fundamental expression, says, "I dislike you or what you've done to the point I wish evil or harm to come to you" or, even worse, "I'd like to be the one to hurt or harm you."

How many people have you hated in your life? I'd say the vast majority of us would say zero. There are people who have taken advantage of all of us. We were angry for what they did. Did we wish them bodily harm because of it? No. There are people who are just not good people. We distance ourselves from them. Do we wish them harm? Of course not. Even the people who have hurt us most deeply: we distance ourselves from them and maybe even wish we'd never known them. But do we wish them harm because of what they've done to us? No.

But there was hate staring me in the face. For the first time in my life, I hated someone so deeply and intensely it penetrated every fiber of my being.

I'd done nothing to bring this situation on myself. I hadn't been out in the clubs carrying on. I hadn't even gone out for a walk in the wrong part of town. I had come, done my business, and kept to myself in my hotel room. I didn't even watch television. I'd just minded my own business. That's it.

Through no fault of my own, these four men had taken me captive. They'd deprived me of all ability to choose for myself. They'd dragged me kicking and screaming through the absolute filth of their world of threats of inhuman acts. They were evil, vile, reprehensible, and I hated them for it.

As that scripture from Matthew played itself over and over in my mind, I thought, *I can't leave this life and have the last feeling I had here on earth be such intense hate. Even more importantly, I can't meet my God with this hate in my heart.* The scripture was clear. I needed to pray for them, and I needed to forgive them. Only then would I be ready to meet God.

If I only had more time. If I could be given a few years to get over this, then I might be able to forgive and pray for them. But now? No matter which way I turned it, what the Lord was asking in this scripture was impossible in this situation. There was no way I could comply with what was required.

These men were going to kill me! Of that I had no doubt. How do you forgive someone who's about to take your life? Oh, sure, you can say, "Okay. I forgive them." But in your heart, you know you don't. It's like being on a diet and telling yourself you're not hungry. You can say it all you want, but it doesn't change the fact that you're still hungry. That's how this was. I could say as many times as I wanted that I forgave these men, but what I really hoped was that somehow these men would get what they had coming in the end.

No. These men were about to kill me, in who knew what kind of gruesome fashion, and there was no way I could forgive them. I couldn't even pray for them. I just couldn't. As much as I knew I should, I couldn't.

It was a dilemma. I was supposed to forgive the unforgivable. Then I thought of Jesus. There he was in the Garden of Gethsemane, on his knees, bleeding at every pore for the weight of the sins He carried—and not just paying the price for the sins but forgiving the very people who were about to take His life. In essence, forgiving the unforgivable.

The problem with that logic is He was Jesus. I was Bob. He had the power to forgive. I didn't. Plain and simple.

Once I realized Jesus could not only forgive the men who had killed him but that He could forgive the men who held me captive, I prayed He would forgive them. I knew it was within His power to do that. If I couldn't forgive them myself, I could at least ask that He forgive them. And I asked that as He did so, His forgiveness would flow through me so I could feel what it felt like to truly forgive someone I hated as much as I hated these men.

Being a person who thinks better "on the move," I realized I had been pacing back and forth in the hotel room for hours.

It's not that I wasn't tired. I was tired—exhausted. But I was far from sleepy.

This hotel room, what most people would call a nondescript hotel room, had become my prison. There was a bed, a desk, and a chair with a lamp behind it. I had sat in the chair many times since my arrival, but I couldn't tell you if it was comfortable or not. It was just a chair.

While pacing back and forth and thinking about forgiveness—both mine and that of my captors—I realized a simple prayer asking God to forgive them was simply not good enough. I had to pray for them with real intent.

I left the phone on the desk and approached the end of the bed. Dropping to my knees with my forearms on the bed, I began to cry unto my God.

Oh, Heavenly Father, I pleaded silently, *I know from everything I've ever been taught that I need to pray for those who despitefully use me. Thou knowest my situation. Thou knowest of my desire to pray for my captors. But thou also knowest the feelings that fill my heart right now. I pray that thou wouldst soften my heart. I pray that thou wouldst help me see them as thou seest them. I pray that I might have strength to pray for them to be turned to thee. Please help me!*

If you're a person who prays, I'm sure you've noticed how some prayers go straight from your mouth to God's ears. Other times you feel they haven't even penetrated the ceiling. Of course, much of what happens depends on the intensity of your prayers. I can promise you my prayers in that situation came directly from the deepest part of my heart and were very intense.

For the next hour, I cried unto God, pleading that He would forgive them and that, somehow, I would feel that. I prayed nearly nonstop. I cried unto Him in the anguish of my soul. I begged Him and pleaded with Him to help me forgive them and to help me desire their well-being. I had read in the scriptures of prophets who'd "wrestled" with God. That's the only word that describes my experience. I wrestled with the Holy Spirit for nearly an hour before the answer came.

Finally, I felt the love of God flow through me to them. I don't know how it happened, and I don't really know how to explain it, but I felt an actual energy enter my body through my left shoulder and flow down through my midsection and out my right hip. It was real. It was tangible. There were atoms flowing there.

And as that happened, a thought came into my understanding: *I have the power and the will to forgive everyone—and so do you. You always have. It's always been there inside you. You just have to unlock it.*

At that point, I began to plead with God again. *Please, Heavenly Father, please help me find that power that is within me. Help me know how to unlock it, that all might be benefitted through it.*

At the very moment I began honestly and diligently seeking that power, I felt the ice in my heart begin to melt. And as it melted, I felt the hatred I felt for these men flee like frost before the rising sun.

Somehow, by the power of God, the hatred was gone. I mean gone! Just like that. I went from intense hatred of these men to a place where I wished them no malice. I felt a sadness for them. They had so debased themselves that their eternal fate was all but sealed. I felt sadness for them, but not hate. I no longer wished them any harm. It was one of the most miraculous things I've ever experienced. In fact, never in my life had I felt the effects of the Atonement of Jesus Christ so powerfully.

Obviously, I was still intimidated by them. It's true I wasn't afraid to die. But it's also true I was really quite afraid of how that might happen. The thought of passing to the other side didn't feel at all bitter. Much to the contrary. After the hell I had been living through for the last seven hours, the sweetness of crossing over into the next life would be welcome. But I was concerned what method they might use to take my life.

And perhaps even more importantly, I worried about how my family would deal with my death. Would they spend the rest of their lives wondering what had happened to me? Would they have to see some horrific account on the news over and over? I think I was really more concerned for them than I was for myself.

And even amidst all these profoundly spiritual experiences I was having, Satan never stopped. His attempts to drag me back down into the pit of despair and gloom with him were absolutely relentless. Just because my burden had been lightened, he never let up—not for a minute. But as time went on, and I regained spiritual and emotional strength. I became more and more able to dismiss his haranguing and to feel the peace of God.

I have read the stories of martyrs who go to their death with a quiet, calm peacefulness. I have often wondered how that could be. And yet here I was. I knew that perhaps I would be dead within the next hour or two, and I felt that same peace and comfort they describe. I'm not saying by any stretch of the imagination that I'm like the martyrs of this or any other age. I'm simply saying I know how they could go forth to their deaths calmly and peacefully. It's a gift from God, and I will always be grateful He gave it to me at this time of such tremendous need.

CHAPTER TEN

SHARING A WITNESS OF JESUS CHRIST

5:00 A.M.
FRIDAY MORNING
FIESTA HOTEL
CHIHUAHUA, MEXICO

HAVING FELT THE FORGIVENESS OF JESUS CHRIST flow through me to my captors, and having found myself no longer hating them, I had the feeling that things were progressing the way they were supposed to. I didn't know what that meant; I just knew that whatever was happening right now was supposed to be happening. In spite of the ever-present, anxiety-fueled fear, I was feeling a measure of peace.

However, I couldn't shake the thought that every time the second hand on the clock hit twelve, I was one minute closer to meeting my maker. It was a sobering thought, and if I dwelled on it too long, it brought a certain sadness and frustration. I may have received a witness from God that He would prepare a place for me with Him, but I just didn't feel ready to leave this life.

The roller coaster continued. I would feel the peace and comfort of the Holy Spirit, which brought a certain quiet to my soul. Then I would consider my imminent demise and start to panic. Then I would remind myself I needed to keep control of my emotions. Then I would pray or read my scriptures and the cycle would begin again.

Somewhere in between all of that, I began to think about the good I had done in my life. As Christians, we spend a great deal of time and energy avoiding doing wrong. But perhaps we don't spend enough time and energy doing good. I started to think about doing something good in what I assumed would be the last few minutes of my life.

I was completely hamstrung, really. I was totally under the control of my captors, so I obviously wasn't free to go out and do some random act of service for someone. I thought about writing a kind letter of appreciation to someone who needed an emotional or spiritual boost, but I was forbidden to have any contact with anyone. My life, for the time being, consisted of me, a nondescript hotel room, and my captor on the phone every three to four minutes.

I started praying to God. *Please, Heavenly Father. If my life is to end, I would like to have at least one more opportunity to do something right—something good.* That prayer was in my heart as I picked up my scriptures.

I turned to 3 Nephi in the Book of Mormon, where I read this verse: "Behold, I am a disciple of Jesus Christ, the Son of God. I have been called of him to declare his word among his people, that they might have everlasting life."

It was plain that God wanted me to declare the redeeming love of Jesus Christ to my captor. I had spent two years of my life serving as a missionary for my church in Guatemala. Every waking hour of every day I had shared that message with those people. I love Jesus Christ, and I love His message. But although I had shared that message with literally thousands of people over the years, I had no idea how to broach the subject with my captor. The relationship was just too out of balance for me to find any degree of normalcy.

I prayed again: *Heavenly Father, I know you want me to share the message of your Son with my captor, and I am willing to do that. I just don't know how. If this is going to happen, you're going to have to direct me. Please help me find a way to open a conversation.*

In just a couple of minutes, my captor came on the speaker phone. I got up out of the chair when I heard his voice and began to pace back and forth in the tiny room.

"*Roberto, estas alli?*" he asked. Are you there?

"*Si,*" I replied. "*Estoy pendiente.*" I'm with you in every way. Then the silence returned. I was going to say something. I wanted to say something—start the conversation. But I didn't know how. *Next time,* I thought. *I'll do it next time he speaks. For sure.*

But the next time came, and the result was exactly the same. He asked if I was there, I said yes, and we drifted back into silence. Then it happened again. I was tongue tied for what may have been the first time in my life. I was a salesman and a negotiator. If anyone knew how to start and carry on a conversation, it was me. But for some reason, I just couldn't make it happen.

Finally, I said to myself, *This is ridiculous! The next time he comes on, you will start a conversation with him no matter how awkward it may seem.*

"Roberto, are you there?" he asked once more in Spanish.

"Yes, I'm here," I replied.

Out of the clear blue sky, a question popped into my mind.

"Do you know how I learned Spanish?" I asked him. I figured he had to wonder, as we had not spoken a single word of English since the whole ordeal had begun seven to eight hours earlier.

"No, how did you learn?" he asked.

"I served as a missionary for my church in Guatemala when I was a young man of nineteen years," I told him. And with that, the flood gates were open. Not only had I opened the door to a conversation in general, but by mentioning my mission, I had opened the door to a religious discussion.

I explained that I had gone to Guatemala to teach the people there about Jesus Christ and how to come unto Him. How they could improve the quality of their lives by living the life He taught. "You know," I told him sincerely, "after two years of teaching those people about Jesus Christ, I learned three things. First, I learned to speak Spanish, which has been a blessing in my life. Second, I learned to truly love the Latino people. In my career I've always worked with Latinos, primarily Mexicans, and I have truly loved them. Third, by teaching people about Jesus Christ, I have come to know Him and to love Him.

"And not only that, two of my sons-in-law have served missions in Mexico. Our whole family speaks Spanish, and we love the culture, and we love the people." I hoped, without being too obvious, that he would realize that as a family we have given much to Mexico.

"Did you baptize anyone on your mission?" he asked.

"Yes, I had the opportunity to baptize many people. It was a blessing to me to be able to see how their lives improved when they began to live the gospel," I told him sincerely.

At that point he asked a question that came completely out of left field: "Do you know Brigham Young?"

I kind of chuckled as I responded. "No. He's been dead for over one hundred years, so I never met him. But I know *of* him, certainly."

He pursued the topic with this question: "Is Joseph Smith still the prophet of your church?"

I wasn't sure how he had connected me with The Church of Jesus Christ of Latter-day Saints. I hadn't said anything about the church. I guess he had seen the missionaries in their slacks, white shirts, ties, and name tags walking around Mexico and had just put two and two together.

I answered his question. "No, Joseph Smith is not the prophet today. He has also passed away. There is another prophet today—a living prophet. Tell me how you know about these things," I said.

"Oh, I've just heard a few things here and there," he said vaguely.

"No way," I responded. "You know more about the church than you're letting on. Tell me how you know."

He hesitated, obviously trying to decide how much to divulge. Finally, he said, "I was baptized into the church as a young man and was an active, practicing member for many years." He paused. "I was a priest in the Aaronic Priesthood and administered the Lord's supper for the people in my congregation."

"Then what?" I asked flabbergasted, wondering how he got from there to where he was today.

"I guess I just drifted away. I started doing things I should have never done. I got involved with people I should never have gotten involved with, and before I knew it, there was no way back."

I felt like I'd just been hit by a semitruck. My captor had been a member of my church at one time in his life? Seriously? This man from whom darkness and evil so profusely flowed had been a member of my church? If he had told me he had arrived on a spaceship from Mars, it would probably have been easier to believe.

At this point, I decided I wasn't going to hold back. This would be the only chance to share with this man that Jesus Christ was mighty to save. And not just with him. I felt like it would be the last time in this life I would have the opportunity to bear witness of the Savior of us all. I decided to tell him and to do it boldly. After all, what could they do? Kill me?

The thought that had been lurking around the edge of my consciousness pushed its way to the center stage of my mind. "Do you know what every one of the people I baptized in Guatemala believed?" I asked him.

"No, what?"

"Every one of them believed God had a plan for them. Do you believe God has a plan for you?"

"Of course not. Why would God care about me in the slightest after all the things I've done?"

"He has a plan for everyone," I told him. "Even you—maybe especially you."

Emboldened by the softness I was feeling from him, I changed directions. "I don't even know who you are. Tell me about you. Tell me your name."

Surprisingly enough, he never hesitated. "My name is Sergio," he said simply. "And I'm smart enough to know that after everything I've done, God does not have a plan for me."

"That's wrong. Satan would have you believe you're beyond the reach of the Atonement of Jesus Christ. But nothing could be further from the truth. The Atonement He made, by shedding His own blood, was an infinite Atonement. Infinite means not you, or anyone else, is beyond its reach."

"That's impossible," he said with some resignation. "You don't understand. I've killed people. I've maimed and mangled people. And I found no remorse in having done so. You're wrong. If God has a plan for me, it is that I burn in hell for the rest of eternity."

"No," I said. "It's you who are wrong. If you could no more than desire to be forgiven, He would draw close to you and show you the way. Nobody is beyond the reach of the Atonement of Jesus Christ. Nobody."

"No," he stated flatly. "It couldn't possibly be. If I know anything, I know I could never be forgiven for what I've done."

At this point I began again to ask why they were holding me. As before, he told me I didn't need to know. All I needed to know was that they had me completely under their control.

Just then, another thought flashed across the screen of my mind. I'd witnessed many times in Guatemala that no matter how evil and foul people might be, they would never harass or harm the missionaries. It was like there was some unwritten rule that you didn't mess with servants of the Lord, or God would bring complete destruction on you. I wondered if that might play to my benefit in this situation.

With that in my mind, I told Sergio, "Sergio, you don't want to hurt me. I am a man of God. I have been a leader in His church. In my responsibility, I directed over three thousand members of His church. God knows me. It will not go well for you if you harm me. Why don't you let me go? You can tell the others I escaped, or whatever you want."

Surprisingly enough, he didn't dismiss the idea out of hand. He said, "You are a man of God. When you speak to me of the things of God, I feel a warmth burning in my chest."

I told him, "That's the Holy Spirit bearing witness to you that what I have said concerning Jesus Christ is true."

"You know, Roberto, I'm completely alone in this world. My family, my friends from my old life, everyone I know, has turned away from me. The people I interact with now . . . I don't have a single person in this life I can trust. I don't know if I could ever be forgiven for all I've done. But if I ever thought I could go to God, I hope that I could find someone like you to help me. Because when you speak to me, I get a really warm feeling in my heart."

I assured him it was indeed possible, and I invited him to apply the atoning blood of Jesus Christ in his life. I invited him once more to let me go. "*No. No se puede*," he responded almost apologetically. It can't be done.

And then, thinking of this lonely, broken man, my heart broke. I felt overwhelmed with compassion as I thought of his sorry life. As thoroughly as my heart had been filled with hatred for this man before, it was now filled with sadness for him. He had once stood in the light and had enjoyed all the blessings for having done so. And now he lived an unspeakably miserable existence where he didn't have one friend—not one single person in his life he could trust.

As we both drifted back into our respective thoughts, I once again fell to my knees on the threadbare carpet at the foot of the bed to thank God for the peace He had sent. I had felt an impression to share the love of Jesus Christ for this man, Sergio, and had done so. And I had done so with boldness and confidence borne of the Spirit. There could be no question in his mind where I stood. I had borne witness several times in our conversation concerning the love of Jesus Christ for him and the forgiveness He was so freely willing to give. There was nothing more I could do than what I had done.

And it stood in stark contrast to how I felt just an hour or two before, facing the prospect of coming into the presence of God with intense hatred in my heart. And within a couple short hours, I had been spiritually transformed to the point I was prepared to come into His presence, having just testified of His Son. What a difference a couple hours and a mighty change of heart had made. I was as ready as I could be to return to that God who had given me life. And I still had the feeling that would be happening soon—very soon.

CHAPTER ELEVEN

HELD FOR RANSOM

7:00 A.M.
FRIDAY MORNING
FIESTA INN HOTEL
CHIHUAHUA, MEXICO

FOR THE NEXT FORTY-FIVE MINUTES, we both slipped back into the routine of silence, each of us in our own private world, our only interaction being Sergio asking if I was there and me responding in the affirmative.

During that time, my mood became what can only be described as melancholy. And even as I say that, it sounds strange to my ears. I don't think I've ever used that word before, but it's interesting how perfectly it fits how I was feeling.

I wasn't particularly afraid. I didn't really feel any anxiety, either. I wasn't numb, just resigned. I felt certain I was going to be killed. I had made my peace with my maker, and all that was left was to just get it over with. The experiences I'd had with the Holy Spirit had bolstered my confidence that I would be okay. It's true these men could end my life. But they couldn't end my existence. My life would continue on another plane—in another sphere, where there would be no pain and no fear.

Looking back now, I would have to say that fatigue also played a key role in how I felt. I hadn't stayed up all night since I was in college. And to go through that kind of emotional and spiritual stress, fear, and anxiety brought me to a state of complete and utter exhaustion. I'd never felt that kind of exhaustion before.

I was beyond sleepy but didn't dare sleep for fear I would be killed for sleeping. My muscles ached from severe tension on the one hand, and almost complete inactivity on the other. But I couldn't even go out and take a little walk in the fresh air to clear my head. My emotions were battered and bruised to the point I could barely put a coherent thought together. My fatigue was so profound I was losing the ability to judge whether my thoughts were even rational.

I was drained, I was exhausted, and I was resigned to whatever fate awaited me. There was still a glimmer of hope out there in the distance that everything would be okay, but it had faded over the last few hours to the point that I could barely even see it flickering anymore.

So the hours from 6:00 a.m. to 7:00 a.m. were basically spent the same way much of the night had been: alternating between sitting in the chair reading my scriptures and kneeling at the foot of the bed in prayer, with a disembodied voice coming to me through the airwaves asking if I was there.

But by this time, even my prayers had diminished in intensity. I had asked all the questions that needed to be asked before I left this earthly existence, and a loving Father had responded. I had prayed for myself, I had prayed for my family, and I had prayed for my captors. All those prayers had been answered. There was no anxiety, no fear, and no urgency left in my prayers. I had received the reassurance I sought, and all that was left was to let the rest of this horrible experience play itself out.

It was shortly after 6:00 a.m. when I felt impressed to add to the note I had left in my scriptures for my family.

> *I shared with my captor that I was a member of the Church and served a mission, and that I love the Latin people and have served them my whole life. I told him my sons-in law both served two-year missions in Mexico. I bore my testimony to the man named Sergio, and he confessed he was a member. A priest in the Aaronic Priesthood at sixteen years old. I told him it was not too late to repent*

and find peace in his life. He told me he doesn't have one person in life that he feels confidence with, but he feels like I would be a person that could help him if he ever found the courage to change his life. I read Third Nephi. I read about having to love those that hurt us. Strangely enough, I can find it in my heart to love him and forgive him. I simply pray that my life will not be over before I can fully prove this forgiveness. If I die, I am not afraid to die but heart-broken that I won't be able to continue being with my family. There are a lot of things in my life that I don't do well enough and could improve on.

They're simple thoughts. But they came from the depths of what had become a soul at peace. I wanted first and foremost for my family to know how much I loved them. I wanted them to know I hadn't gone to the other side of the veil with hatred in my heart for my captors. I wanted them to have some sense of the spiritual transformation I had gone through. I read these words today and see the grammatical errors and wonder why I didn't say this or say that. But when I consider where I was physically, emotionally, and spiritually at that particular moment in time, I'm surprised it conveys the thoughts that were in my heart as clearly as it does.

As I was pondering these things, I was interrupted by Sergio's voice on the phone. I knew the second I heard his voice, something had changed—drastically. During our conversation earlier, his voice had begun to soften. I could see his humanity. But in this moment, his voice was filled with anger, hate, and most of all, evil. The contrast was simply shocking.

My first thought was sadness that Satan had dragged him back into the pit. My next feeling was intimidation and fear. The fear I had felt earlier in the evening had gradually dissipated throughout the night. But just like flipping a switch, it was back with a vengeance. I could feel the absolute danger in his voice, and the warning alarms in my head were ringing at a volume that was almost unbearable.

"I'm going to ask you some questions," he said. "And I want

you to think before you answer. If you lie to me—about anything or to any degree—I will know it, and we will kill you immediately. I want the straight-up truth. Anything else will result in a death you can't imagine."

His voice dripped with evil, and there was no question in my mind that this man was capable of literally anything!

"What is it you want to know?" I asked.

"What is your wife's name?" he demanded.

My heart stopped beating, and I froze in fear. I was in the middle of this, and there was no way out. I had accepted that. But there was no way I was going to let them drag my wife and children into this. If they killed me, it would be my fault for choosing to come to Mexico in the first place. But there was absolutely no way I was going to let them drag my family into this.

"Why do you need my wife's name?" I asked, trying to buy some time.

"I just need to verify you are telling me the truth," he responded with an unspoken threat in his voice.

If indeed this was a test and I didn't give the correct name, he would know I was lying and bring some unspeakable form of death down upon me. On the other hand, if he didn't have my wife's name yet and I gave it to him, I might be signing her death warrant. I may have become resigned to my own death, but the thought of my family being killed, or tortured, or who can even imagine what, at the hands of these ravening wolves was unbearable.

The thought quickly jumped into my mind to use a name similar to my wife's name—a name I could claim was a nickname if they called me on it. My wife's name is Lynnette, but there was no way I was going to share her real name with them. If they killed me because of it, then so be it, but there was no way I could do that to my wife. The name Linda flashed into my mind, and it was close enough to Lynette that I went with it.

For the first time in this whole ordeal, I felt I had no other choice than to take a chance.

"Her name is Linda," I said as convincingly as I could.

There was a pause. *That choice to lie just cost me my life,* I thought. *I shouldn't have lied. I should have told the truth.*

"Okay," he said. "What is your position in your company?"

What? He'd accepted the name? The door wasn't going to come crashing in at any minute?

I continued. "I'm nobody in my company. Just someone who speaks Spanish. They told me they would pay me a couple hundred dollars extra if I would come and inspect the produce here."

"You're lying," he said, venom dripping from his words.

Yes, I was. Plainly. And the problem was, I'm not a good liar. I don't ever lie. My mother taught me that you tell the truth and you take your lumps, whatever they might be. I had learned that lesson very painfully at a very young age and had lived it my whole life.

The scene flashed across the screen of my mind like a bullet train racing across the countryside, but it was so clear it was as though I was living it again. I was at the small-town grocery store with my mother as a young child. There was some penny candy in a tote near the checkout, and I put several pieces in my pocket. When we got home, my mother said, "Bobby, where did you get that candy?" I looked her right in the eye and said, "I had some money and I bought it while we were at the store."

My mother knew I had no money, and she knew I didn't buy it. But unlike what some of us might have done, she didn't rant, she didn't rave, and she didn't even raise her voice. We sat on the couch, and she put her arm around me. Quietly, gently even, she said, "Bobby, you didn't have any money, did you? You didn't buy that candy; you stole it. Didn't you?" As I looked up into my mother's eyes, I could see the disappointment there. "We're not thieves, Bobby. We pay our way, and we never take what's not ours. And we always, always tell the truth, no matter how hard that might be."

That's all it took, and the flood gates opened. Those few moments, sitting on the couch with my mother speaking to me lovingly and kindly, her arm around me, had a more powerful impact on my life than any amount of punishment could have had. I knew she was right. I knew what she'd said was true. I should have never done it. And I knew I shouldn't have done it while I was doing it, but somehow I got swept down a path I knew I shouldn't have been on in the first place.

If I live to be a hundred years old, I will never forget the disappointment in my mother's eyes. She loved me, and I loved her. I knew I never wanted to disappoint her again. In that moment, I committed myself to being honest. I would never steal anything again as long as I lived, and I would never lie. It just wasn't worth it.

The little scene played out in my mind. We went back to the grocery store and talked to the owner and paid him for the candy I had stolen. I didn't want to return to the store—not after what I had done. But a wise mother took the opportunity to teach me that repentance for sin involves being accountable for what happened. That accountability manifests itself in confession. The owner of the store was a kind, older man who sat with me and helped me understand why what I did was wrong. Just like my mother, he didn't rant, he didn't rave. He just sat quietly with me, explaining why it was wrong to steal. He was such a kind and gentle man. I will never forget him.

So, because of that one powerful experience as a little boy, I never lie to anyone and, frankly, the words stuck in my throat as I said them. I suppose that's what he felt when he accused me of lying. But the die was cast, and my only hope was to see it through.

"Why would I lie? I have nothing to gain by lying. I came to look at the farming operation so I could earn a few hundred extra dollars."

"No," he said. "You're important enough that your company will pay for you. This is about the money. This has always been about the money. You're doing business in Mexico, and your company will show respect to the cartels."

"How much do you want?" I asked.

"Why do you always have so many questions?" he shot back. "You don't ask the questions around here, we do."

I sensed the anger in his voice. This was not a man you wanted to make angry.

"What would you have me do?" I asked submissively.

"You need to make preparations to make a ransom demand from your company."

"What will I need to do to make those preparations?" I asked.

"Listen very carefully," he directed. "One mistake and you're dead."

He went on to explain how I was to go to an OXXO convenience store down the street on the corner and buy a disposable cell phone. I would then use that phone to call my company and make the ransom demand. He told me they had placed people all along the way from the hotel to the convenience store, and if I tried to run, or talk to anyone, or anything like that, I would immediately be scooped up and killed.

What in the world was a disposable cell phone? And why would I look for such a thing at a convenience store, of all places? How did the phone work? Would they want ID to set it up? Would I pay with my credit card? There were a thousand questions spilling out of my mind, all of which I didn't dare ask. He had been very forceful in pointing out that they asked the questions and I answered them. I could only hope that when I got to OXXO, the person there would know what I was talking about.

I was instructed to walk out the front door of the hotel and turn left. As I walked out of my room, I expected to feel a measure of freedom at being out in the open—but nothing could be further from the truth. I felt a huge wave of anxiety wash over me. It was so intense I wanted to go back into the room. As I walked through the lobby of the hotel and out the front door onto the sidewalk, I looked at everyone with suspicion. It was so hard to tell who might be with the cartel and who wasn't. It was nearly 7:00 a.m. and the sun was up, the city was awake, and people were out and about. I walked down the street, careful not even to brush up against anyone. I didn't want to accidentally start something.

I could see the bright orange-and-red sign of the OXXO store across the street and waited for an opening in the traffic so I could cross. Then I heard Sergio's voice over the phone.

"Do you see those two guys sitting on the park bench across from the store?" he asked.

"I see them," I responded.

"They are our men. They can see every move you make, both inside and outside the store. If you make one wrong move, they will kill you where you stand. Do you understand?"

I indicated I understood.

"You're not going to do anything stupid, are you?" he asked.

"No, I'm not. I'm just going to go inside, buy the phone, and go straight back to the hotel."

"I hope so," he said. "For your sake."

I've got to quit shaking, I thought as I approached the desk. Normally you just tell yourself to get a grip and you're okay. But I was so tired and so emotionally spent I was afraid anyone looking at me would know something wasn't right. I certainly didn't want to have that conversation with anyone.

The store was busy with the morning rush-hour traffic, and it took me some time to get up to the counter. When I finally got there, I asked the girl for the cell phone. Thankfully, she knew what I was talking about and got it for me. She told me all I had to do was install the SIM card and the phone was good to go. The problem was, I didn't know what a SIM card was or that phones even had them, let alone how one might be installed.

Panic began to overtake me. I could see a situation where I got back to the hotel and couldn't make the phone work. I know how to work electronic devices, but I don't consider myself particularly tech savvy. I told the girl at the desk, "You're going to have to help me install this card and make sure it works. I don't know how."

She began to help me put it in, but there were a ton of customers behind me. She said, "Let me help these people, then I'll help you with the phone." I stepped aside.

After just a minute or two, Sergio's voice was on the phone. "Take the phone off speaker and put it up to your ear," he said menacingly.

When I had done that, he said, "What are you doing in there? This is ridiculous. You knew you were supposed to go straight in there, buy the phone, and leave. You're stalling. Do I have to have those two men from across the street come in there and get you? Get moving!"

"I don't know how these phones work," I said with some exasperation. "I've never even seen one of these phones. We don't have them in the States. If this girl doesn't help me set this up, it will never work. I'm hurrying. She's almost done."

"Put the phone back on speaker," he said, angrily. "And hurry up!"

About that time, the girl was free for a minute and took my new phone and got everything organized. It was only a minute or two and I was out of there. I looked over to the park bench, and the two guys were gone. I wondered as I hurried back to the hotel if they were behind me the whole way. I didn't dare turn around to look. Maybe I didn't want to know.

Safely back in my room, I breathed a sigh of relief.

8:15 A.M.
FRIDAY MORNING
FIESTA INN HOTEL
CHIHUAHUA, MEXICO

"I want you to listen carefully," Sergio said over the phone. "You're going to call your company, and you're going to say exactly what I tell you. If you deviate from what I tell you even one word, it will be the last word you ever speak. Do you understand?"

He then went on to tell me what I would say. I would ask for Trevor, the CFO of our company, and tell him I was being held against my will in Mexico, that they would need to pay a ransom for my freedom, and that I would call later to tell them how much, when, where, and how.

Having rehearsed with them several times what I was going to say, I put my newly acquired cell phone on speaker and dialed the number of my office in Utah. One of the sales assistants, Enaka, answered the call.

"This is Bob," I said. "I need to talk to Trevor immediately. If he's busy or on the phone, please interrupt him."

She said okay and transferred the call.

Unbeknownst to me, she went and alerted Trevor of my call and came back into the "bullpen," where she and all the salesmen worked, and said, "That was Bob. Something's not right."

Trevor answered and said, "Hey, Bob. What's up?"

I said, "Trevor, I'm being held against my will in Mexico."

Before I could continue, I heard him chuckle. "Sure you are, Bob. When will you be home?"

According to the script, I continued. "They are demanding a ransom. I will contact you soon to let you know how much and how to make the transfer. In the meantime, you get everything ready on your end." With that, I hung up as instructed.

CHAPTER TWELVE

THE RANSOM AMOUNT

8:30 A.M.
FRIDAY MORNING
FIESTA INN HOTEL
CHIHUAHUA, MEXICO

QUITE FRANKLY, AT THIS POINT I WAS RELIEVED. And I don't mean just a little relieved. All night long I had carried the burden of not knowing why I was being held. And when you don't know what's going on, your mind starts building up worst-case scenarios until you've fully explored some very, very ugly possibilities.

This whole thing was all about money? That's what Sergio had said—all about the money. That was it? Just money? It wasn't a random act of terror? It wasn't some sort of political statement where I would be the punch line? It was just money? It was like I had stepped from the darkest night into the brightest day. Only two things had to happen, and I was home free—find out how much and find out how to get it to them. How hard could that be?

I had been instructed not to ask so many questions, so I just waited for them to tell me how much. I knew it wouldn't be long. In my mind I was going through every possible scenario of how to raise the money. If it was a few thousand dollars, I could handle that out of my personal finances. If it was a few tens of thousands, that would harder but still doable. If it was a few hundreds of thousands, it would be very difficult. If they wanted millions, I was a dead man.

About that time, my captors came back on the phone. Sergio was no longer the spokesperson. And even though he had let evil overtake him once again, I was sorry to see him hand the phone off to another. He was still the least vile of the four men. But this time it was someone else.

"Roberto, are you there?" he asked in Spanish, breaking the silence.

"Yes, I'm here."

"Good. Listen very carefully. You need to call your company again and tell them they need to be prepared to send $300,000 . . ."

I don't know if he paused there, but time simply stopped dead in its tracks. In that millisecond, I thought, How are we going to come up with $300,000? As CEO, I knew my company didn't have that kind of cash lying around. No company does. I knew I couldn't pull together that much out of my personal finances without refinancing my house or liquidating investments, all of which would take way too long.

The light I had been basking in suddenly started to dim again.

". . . pesos," my captor continued.

Pesos? Had he just said pesos? I quickly did the math in my head. At just over fifteen pesos to the dollar, three hundred thousand pesos amounted to just under twenty grand. Wait. Did I understand that right? They had kidnapped me, held me against my will, and terrorized me for more than twelve hours for $20,000?

The light began to grow brighter again. I thought, *Gee, if it's only $20,000, I could write him a check and be home by* *noon.* Of course, I don't carry my checkbook with me, and they probably wouldn't take a check anyway, but $20,000 was certainly within reach for my company and even for my family.

I was halfway there. I knew the amount, and the amount presented no obstacle. We just had to come up with an acceptable way to get them the money, and my life would likely be spared. All night long I had sunk deeper and deeper into a bottomless pit of despair, thinking there was no way my life would possibly be spared. For the first time in twelve very long hours, I thought, *I might just get out of this alive.*

Caution immediately plunged in and said, *Not so fast, buddy. This could all fall apart at any time.* Maybe so. But for the first time, there was at least a chance I might get through this unscathed. Maybe it wasn't such a huge chance, but when you've convinced yourself—or been convinced by the cartel—that you're going to die a horrible death, even an infinitesimally small chance of survival is immensely appealing.

I knew I'd been commanded not to ask questions, but the hope that had suddenly started growing in my soul broke forth: "I think we can do this without too much difficulty. We could do an electronic transfer from the US. You'll have your money this afternoon. What account would you like it sent to?"

"Stop!" my captor demanded. "You don't tell us how this will go. We tell you."

There I was again—right back in my place.

"You're going to call your company and have them get the money together. Then someone from your company is going to put that cash in a briefcase, get on a plane, and hand carry that money to Chihuahua. That employee will give you the briefcase, and you will leave him and bring the money to us."

Seriously? I started thinking maybe I had underestimated how easy it was going to be to get them the money. But when he talked about asking someone from my company to put their life at risk coming to Mexico to bring the money, my heart missed several beats. There was no way I could ask anyone to do that. I knew without question if that was the only acceptable method of delivering the cash, I would die today.

And it wasn't just putting my coworkers at risk that had my heart racing. They still wanted to use me as the pawn in all this. I could see the whole scenario in my mind: someone would give me the money, and I would go to some agreed-upon, out-of-the-way place in the country where they would take the briefcase and put a bullet in my head. That was how these things went. How many times had they already threatened to do exactly that? I knew they were capable of doing it, and I knew that after I had seen them face-to-face, they'd have no option but to kill me. To let me go would be lunacy. These people were cold, calculating, professional terrorists, but they were not lunatics. Shooting me in the back of the head as I walked away would cause them no remorse whatsoever. They had done that sort of thing so many times they wouldn't even give it a second thought.

No. This proposal was impossible from whatever way you chose to look at it. I couldn't let it happen. Period. I wouldn't let it happen.

"That's impossible," I argued as pointedly as I dared. I still knew who held the power in this relationship. I still knew what they were capable of. But there was no way this was going to happen. If it cost me my life, I wouldn't even share this option with my friends back in the United States.

"There's no way an employee would ever get out of the States with a briefcase full of cash. Homeland security x-rays every bag. When they see that someone is taking a large sum of cash on a flight to Mexico, they'll detain that person. It looks too much like money laundering. Where would we be, then? The United States government would have your cash. You don't want that. I don't want that either. What else can I say? There's no way this plan can work."

There was silence on the other end of the line. Had I played my hand too vigorously? Were they on the way up to my room to kill me for insubordination? My mind started running amok.

"Okay," the man from the cartel said. "You're going to make another call to your company to let them know the amount. We will decide how to make the money change hands and let you know. When you call your money guy, here's what you'll say . . ."

He went on to explain that I'd tell Trevor the amount was three hundred thousand pesos, which amounted to $20,000, and that he should be ready to send that amount by the means we would specify in the next call. I was then to hang up. After that, we role-played it several times, and once they were satisfied, we made the call.

The captor who was currently on the phone didn't like the idea of going through my company switchboard again, so he asked me what Trevor's cell phone number was. When I gave it to him, he told me to call Trevor direct.

CHAPTER THIRTEEN

EVENTS IN UTAH

8:30 A.M.
FRIDAY MORNING
ONIONS 52 OFFICE
SYRACUSE, UTAH

MY COMMENTS

WITH MY FIRST PHONE CALL TO MY OFFICE IN UTAH, the anxiety and stress I had been suffering for the last twelve hours was suddenly thrust upon everyone in my office. That was especially true for those most closely involved.

I think rather than try to relate the feelings of those friends and coworkers in Utah, I'll let you hear their side of the story firsthand. First, we'll hear from Trevor, who was the first person I called. Later, we'll hear from my good friend Shawn and my wife.

TREVOR'S STORY

I THINK FOR ME, THE BEST PLACE TO START is the day before Bob left for Texas. The management team had gathered in the conference room to go over some last-minute details. As is often the case, the meeting was upbeat and positive. Toward the end of the meeting, Bob announced that if he was able to conclude his business in Texas on time, he was considering going to visit the new grower in Mexico.

As it was the first time anyone in our company had been to this part of Mexico, and it is known as a dangerous area, we started joking about Bob being careful that he didn't get kidnapped. One of the management team said, "Well, whatever you do, don't get kidnapped." Everyone laughed.

I said, "Yeah, because we're not going to pay the ransom if you do."

There was some lighthearted banter back and forth, but Bob seemed comfortable going to Mexico, so we sort of took our cue from him. Nobody seemed terribly concerned.

It was just after eight o'clock in the morning the day Bob was supposed to be coming home when our sales assistant, Enaka, rang through to my office and told me she had Bob on the line. She then came into my office to make sure I had the taken the call. I took the call, wondering why he wasn't already on the plane home and why he hadn't just called my cell phone.

When he told me he'd been kidnapped, I didn't really know what to think. If somebody had walked into my office and hit me in the face with a two-by-four, I wouldn't have been any more floored by what I heard.

"Trevor, it's Bob. I'm being held against my will by the cartel in Mexico, and they are demanding a ransom. I will call you with the amount and instructions shortly."

With that announcement, he hung up.

I didn't believe him at first. I thought he was continuing the joke of the other day. However, something pierced my heart, and I knew what he was saying was true.

For the first minute or so after the call ended, I sat nailed to my chair. Was that real? Did Bob just tell me in all seriousness that he'd been kidnapped? My first thought was that he would call right back and say, "Oh, I got you. You swallowed that one hook, line, and sinker!" But he didn't call right back. I waited for a minute, half expecting the call, but it never came.

After a minute or so, I walked out into the sales area. "Bob's been kidnapped," I announced to the group. "He's being held against his will, and they are demanding a ransom."

The initial reaction I got from the sales floor was about the same as the reaction Bob got from me. "Okay. What's the punch line?" someone said. But much the same way I could tell Bob was serious by the tone of his voice, they quickly realized I wasn't pranking them.

It was about that time my cell phone rang. The caller ID said, "Chihuahua, Mexico" and my heart jumped up in my throat. I went into my office to take the call.

8:45 A.M.
FRIDAY MORNING
FIESTA INN HOTEL
CHIHUAHUA, MEXICO

AS TREVOR'S PHONE RANG, I COULDN'T HELP BUT HOPE I hadn't endangered his life in some way by giving out his personal cell phone number. Obviously, he could change the number when all this wound down, but I sincerely hoped and prayed he wasn't at any undue risk because I had given the cartel his private number.

I also hoped that when he saw how small the amount was, he would feel the same relief I had felt. Finally, I sincerely hoped there would be no problem in raising the money. I knew the money was there. I couldn't imagine any reason for any kind of holdup on their end, but none of us had ever been in this kind of situation. My anxiety was back to a fever pitch. My freedom was close enough to reach out and grab ahold of, and yet it was still light-years away.

Trevor answered his phone on the third ring. "Hello?" he said cautiously.

"Trevor, this is Bob again. Listen carefully and write this down. The ransom amount is three hundred thousand pesos, which is just under $20,000. You need to pull that much cash together and be ready to send it when I call again with instructions as to where and how. I will call again soon."

"Bob, do I need to call the cops?" Trevor asked.

"No. There's no need to involve the cops. Just get the money as quickly as you can."

With that, I hung up the phone. Trevor was a good man. I felt confident he would do what needed to be done.

I knew this whole thing would be stressful for my friends and coworkers, but I also knew that having the demands out in the open would help everyone cope—everyone, including me. Somewhere in the back of my mind I felt an impression that transferring the money wasn't going to be the slam dunk I was hoping for. I chased the thought away, but like a bad cold, it kept returning.

CHAPTER FOURTEEN

A FLURRY OF ACTIVITY

9:00 A.M.
FRIDAY MORNING
ONIONS 52 OFFICE
SYRACUSE, UTAH

TREVOR'S STORY

ONCE AGAIN, I SAT AT MY DESK. It was like the world was slowing down. Or like I was having an out-of-body experience. Was that really Bob on the phone? Yes. Of course. There was no question it was him. But there was something different about his voice. Bob is always so upbeat, almost playful. He is positive about everything, and it's always a lift to talk to him.

But in this case there was something different about his whole demeanor. He was very serious—almost solemn, emotionless. It was like an automaton of Bob. But there was no question it was him. There was no hint of any playfulness or positivity. He got straight to the point and gave me his message clearly and succinctly. There were no pleasantries and no chitchat. He got right to the point, said what he had to say, and hung up. That was so unlike him.

Bob was kidnapped! Were we ever going to see him again? Was the last time we saw him the last time we would ever see him? On the one hand it didn't seem real. I kept waiting to wake up with a shiver and say, "I'm glad that was just a dream."

But on the other hand, it was all too real. Bob was my friend, and he was in trouble. He'd called me. I knew he was counting on me. But what could I do? I wasn't in Mexico. I was hundreds of miles away from Mexico, safe in my office in Utah. What could I do? The rapidly-growing, cold, aching lump in the pit of my stomach told me this wasn't going to end well.

I realized the first thing I could do was go and do exactly as Bob had instructed me. If Bob was to have any chance of making it through this, we would have to do our part, with no mistakes.

The first thing I did was gather the owners in the conference room and explain what the ransom demands were. It took all of about eight seconds for everyone to agree we would pay the ransom. Twenty thousand dollars was something we could manage easily enough. From there, Shawn and I walked back out into the sales area we called the bullpen and started making assignments.

We assigned a person to call our personal representative at the bank and let him know I would be coming in and to have $20,000 in twenty dollar bills ready to go. Bob had said not to contact the police, but who else was there to help us get Bob back? We decided we had no choice but to call.

We assigned a person to call the local police. We assigned yet another to get in touch with the FBI in Salt Lake City to get them involved. Another was assigned to go through Bob's credit card charges and make a call to the hotel in Mexico to see if Bob had checked out. We had another person calling the airlines to see if Bob had boarded his flight this morning. The office was a flurry of activity. The bullpen was buzzing like a hive of angry bees when I left for the bank. For the time being, at least, we had shifted out of selling-onions mode and into lifesaving mode.

When I got to the bank, our banker met me at the door. He had everything almost ready. He had me sit down in front of his desk and explained what was happening on his end. I told him everything I knew about Bob, which, frankly, wasn't much at this point. But our banker was genuinely concerned for Bob's safety and was very helpful.

You never know how a banker might react when you tell him straight up you are sending thousands of dollars in cash to a cartel in Mexico, but if he was concerned about it, he didn't let on. He was very kind and accommodating. I was only in the bank for a few short minutes when they brought a bag containing $20,000 in twenty-dollar bills. In most ways, it was just like any other transaction. They set the zippered money pouch on the desk. I signed the receipt, and I walked out with the money—money I hoped would save the life of my friend.

Arriving back at the office, I got the news I was dreading: Bob hadn't checked out of the hotel, hadn't caught his flight, and, almost certainly, was in the grasp of the cartel, just like he had said. The bad feeling that had been growing inside me ratcheted up to the next level.

About that time, the local police arrived. To say they were unhelpful would be a huge understatement. They laughed and joked and didn't take anything we said seriously. It wasn't long before we told them we would take it from here and asked them to leave.

In their defense, this was probably the first kidnapping call they'd ever received. Kidnappings simply don't happen in a sleepy little Utah town. And when you complicate it by telling them it's an international kidnapping, it's way out of their realm of expertise.

We had gotten in touch with the FBI, and after having our call transferred from person to person for over half an hour, we finally had someone who took us seriously and told us they'd get to our location as quickly as possible. Their office was a good hour or more from ours, but at least they were on the way.

I no idea what to do and no experience with anything even close to this situation. They don't teach a course on international kidnapping in MBA school. This sort of thing just never happens to real people. And yet I felt personally responsible for the outcome. I was suddenly being held accountable for someone's life, yet there was basically nothing I could do to influence the outcome.

CHAPTER FIFTEEN

COMING UP WITH A PLAN

9:30 A.M.
FRIDAY MORNING
FIESTA INN HOTEL
CHIHUAHUA, MEXICO

AFTER REALIZING THERE WAS NO WAY THEIR FIRST PLAN could work, my captors put me on hold. I assume they had muted their phone, because I couldn't hear anything from their end. And while the silence made me somewhat uneasy after being in near-constant communication for the last twelve hours, it brought relief.

In the last couple hours, everything had changed. It's true I had prayed unceasingly throughout the night and those prayers had a purpose. I was almost certain I would be killed, and my prayers were centered on preparing myself for what would inevitably come. But now everything was different.

Up until three hours ago I couldn't see anything but my death. Now I could see a way out. There was a possibility, however slim, that I might get out of this alive. I felt like it was possible that if I could find a way to get them their money while at the same time keeping myself out of harm's way, they might let me go. That slim sliver of hope was exhilarating to my battered psyche.

And so my prayers changed. While I had been praying to be spiritually prepared when the time came, I was now praying I could return to those I loved. As I had gotten myself "right" with God, the intensity of my prayers had diminished. Now I was back on my knees pleading for a door leading to my release to be opened. I knew it was possible. I also knew it wasn't probable. But that tiniest glimmer of hope had renewed my energy, and my prayers returned to full intensity.

What my captors had taken from me during the night was hope. As long as you have hope, you're in the fight. When all hope is extinguished, you have nothing but resignation and despair. I had avoided that despair through faith that I would be returning to the loving Heavenly Father who had given me life, but I had totally resigned myself to the hopelessness of my situation.

And yet here it was! Hope! It's absolutely astounding what the slightest possibility of hope—no matter how far in the future—can do for your spirits.

After what felt like a lifetime, my captors came back on the phone. I guess the most important thing from their perspective was to keep me in my place.

"This is ridiculous!" my captor shouted, shattering the silence. "If you want to get out of this alive, you'd better stop being so difficult."

"I'm not being difficult," I responded. "I want this as badly as you do. Just give me the number of your bank account here in Mexico. You'll have your money in twenty minutes, and this can all be over."

"What are you talking about?" he thundered. "We don't have a bank account number. Here's how this is going to go. You are going to call your company and have them send the money to a bank here in Chihuahua. You will leave the hotel, go to the bank, show them your ID, and collect the money. You'll bring the money to us at an agreed-upon location, and that will be that."

Here we go again, I thought. *Not only is it impossible for my bank to send money to a "bank" with no account number, they are still trying to put me in the same untenable situation.*

"That's impossible," I said with a confidence that belied my fear. "Banks don't send money to banks. Money is sent from one bank account to another bank account. You can't just send money to a bank. The receiving bank has to have a place to put it. And even if a bank was willing to receive the money, there's no way they're going to let some gringo waltz in and collect a large sum of money they just received. If, for some miraculous reason, they decided to do a deal like that, they would hold the money for at least a week, maybe more. There isn't a bank in Chihuahua that would let something like this happen. No way."

"What did I tell you about being difficult?" he roared into the phone. "Hold on. I'll be right back."

Once again I feared I might have come on too strong. What I had said was true—every word of it—but pushing it back in his face might not have been the best idea. Sometimes you just can't tell. If you come on as weak, they treat you as weak and you get the worst. It's also possible, on the other hand, to come on too strong. They might respect you if you come on strong, but if it's too strong, you're dead.

I was walking the razor's edge. I wanted to appear strong and competent; I didn't want to appear pushy and arrogant. But that line is only determined in the eyes of the beholder. I had no choice but to take my chances.

As we progressed through all of this, the one thing that was becoming apparent was that these people were experts in terrorism but complete novices in the financial world. On the one hand, this was the first sign of weakness I had seen in them. But weakness is probably the wrong word. I suspect anyone ever having the displeasure to encounter one of these men would never use the word *weak*. It wasn't weakness. It was simply that either they had never done this before or they hadn't taken the time to think it all the way through this time around. That tiny glimmer of hope I had been hanging on to just got ever so slightly brighter.

It was a long fifteen minutes or more before they came back on the line.

"This is taking way too long," he said, once again breaking the silence. "This is how this is going to go, and we don't care what you think. Western Union will send up to $1,000 to anywhere from anywhere with no questions asked. You are going to call your company right now and explain to them that they need to have twenty people each go to Western Union and send $950 to twenty people on this end, whose names we will provide."

I liked it! For the first time since they had told me they were holding me for ransom, they had floated a plan that didn't have me squarely in the crosshairs. People here in Chihuahua would collect the money, not me. It was slick, it was clean, and I could see no reason it wouldn't work—although I didn't bother to share that, since they didn't care what I thought this time.

I knew my company had $20,000 available, I knew they would send it, I knew these men could find people here to pick up the money, and I knew I wasn't in the line of fire. Once again, my flicker of hope grew brighter.

"We're going to call your money guy and tell him how this is going to go. Here's what you're going to say . . ."

As we had done all morning long, we rehearsed what I would say and then role-played it until I could go all the way through it to their satisfaction. Then we made the call.

"Hello?" It was Trevor's voice.

"Trevor, it's Bob. Here is how this is going to play out. Write this down. There can't be any mistakes. You are going to find twenty people and give each of them $950 in cash. You will instruct them to go straight to Western Union there in Utah and send the money to Chihuahua. I will be sending you a list of the names of the recipients. This needs to be done as quickly as possible for my sake. No mistakes."

With that, I broke the connection. The only word Trevor had spoken was hello.

I knew Trevor was smart, and I knew he was responsible. It wouldn't have surprised me if he would have had a $20,000 pile of hundred-dollar bills sitting on his desk when I called back. I could count on Trevor. I had only known Trevor for a few months, but he was one of those people you just knew you could count on.

I also knew I could count on my friend Shawn. I had known Shawn for decades, and we had always had each other's back. Shawn was one of the owners of Onions 52 and, after years of trying, was responsible for finally convincing me to come to the company just six months earlier. Yes, Shawn and I had been friends long enough there was no question in my mind he would be there for me no matter what.

Really, I knew I could count on everyone I worked with. We were like a family, and we watched out for each other. Not only did that fact bring me peace, it gave me strength to take steps I would shortly have to take. The best thing was I could actually see a scenario where I might actually live through this and my spirit began to soar.

Going over possible scenarios in my mind, I couldn't help but see the obvious. I'd never seen my captors. I couldn't identify any of them. I didn't know where they were calling from. Caller ID in Mexico is not what it is here in the States. For all I knew, they could have been in Mexico City. I could be of no help whatsoever in their capture or prosecution. Undoubtedly, they knew that as well.

With those thoughts in mind, I could see no reason for them to kill me. There was no reason whatsoever not to release me once they had their money. I suppose they could have continued to hold me and start the whole process over, but that was a long shot. The longer they held me, the more at risk they were. I knew they didn't want that.

No. The logical thing to do after they'd gotten what they wanted was to just break the phone connection and go spend their money. It made sense for them to let me go. That's what I wanted, and it seemed reasonable that was just what could happen. As had been steadily happening for the last hour or so, my optimism for my immediate future grew cautiously brighter.

How hard could it be to get twenty people, go down to Western Union, and send the money?

CHAPTER SIXTEEN

WESTERN UNION

10:00 A.M.
FRIDAY MORNING
ONIONS 52 OFFICE
SYRACUSE, UTAH

TREVOR'S STORY

SUDDENLY MY PHONE RANG AGAIN. It was Bob.

"Here's how this will go. I assume you have the money. If not, you need to get it as quickly as possible. Once you have the money, you will take it to the Western Union office, and you will send $950 to twenty people whose names you will receive shortly. The money needs to be sent from twenty different people on your end. I have given the cartel Shawn's cell phone number. The cartel wants a Spanish speaker to answer Shawn's phone next time we call. They will give all the routing information to him. In the meantime, you go to Western Union and be ready to send the money when they send the contact information. Do you understand?" With my affirmative reply, he broke the connection.

10:30 A.M.
FRIDAY MORNING
WESTERN UNION OFFICE
CLINTON, UTAH

SHAWN'S STORY

I GUESS I WOULD HAVE TO START MY STORY thirty-plus years ago. I met Bob when I was just a young man. Even though I was young and inexperienced in life, I knew Bob Meek was someone I could trust. He was a man of the highest integrity. He treated me like an equal, even though I was more than ten years his junior, and I loved him for that. Our families have been close friends for decades.

Over the years I tried many times to get Bob to come to work with us. He is well-known and highly respected in the produce business, and I knew he would be an asset to our team. But up until about six months before this whole ordeal began, we had never been able to make it work. But now we had finally convinced him to join us, and he had already made a huge contribution to our success.

That morning, when Trevor walked into the sales area and announced Bob had been kidnapped, I didn't believe him. I thought he was joking. We're all friends in our office, and jokes seem to make the day pass in a more pleasant way. But it quickly became apparent Trevor wasn't joking. Even though I could see he was serious, I couldn't believe it. Maybe I didn't want to believe it.

Suddenly I was buried by an avalanche of guilt. I had let Bob to go to Mexico to check out this new grower. He had only been with us for a few months, and I felt like he was in a situation where he might lose his life. How could he ever forgive me? How could his family ever forgive me for what I had let him do? Most importantly, how could I ever forgive myself for putting the life of this man I admired so much in this type of situation? What was I even thinking?

As I was sitting there pondering this terrible thing I had done, the phone rang. I looked down at the caller ID, and it said the call was from Mexico. Bob told Trevor the ransom was $20,000 and that he would send instructions.

Within just a few minutes, my cell phone rang. I could see from the caller ID it was from Mexico. It was Bob.

"Shawn, from now on, my captors will contact the company on your cell phone. They want a Spanish speaker on the line when they call. They want to be sure you have an app on your cell phone called WhatsApp. They will use your phone and that app to communicate. Do you understand?"

I told him I did, and the line went dead.

Bob didn't sound good. I mean, I guess he sounded fine. It was clearly Bob, but then again, it wasn't the Bob I knew so well. The hollowness in his voice increased the fear that had gripped my soul and wouldn't let go.

First I checked my phone. Yes, WhatsApp was still there. That took me to the issue of having a Spanish speaker to deal with these people. We have many people who speak some Spanish in our company. You don't spend your life in the produce business without learning at least a little Spanish. But for this situation, I felt we needed a native Spanish speaker. We had many Latin people working in our plant, and I picked one in whom I had a great deal of confidence. His name was Mario.

I invited Mario into my office and explained the situation to him. He looked at the floor and could hardly talk. I thought at first it was because of how he felt about Bob, but there was more—much more.

Mario was of Mexican descent. He had grown up there, not far from where Bob was being held. He was all too aware of the danger. I remembered that his brother had been killed by the cartels in a particularly violent fashion. One year later, they'd killed his brother's wife as well. Whenever Mario returns to

Mexico, he goes to his small hometown. But he never makes a big public appearance. He just enjoys his family in their small, humble home.

I knew that asking for Mario's help would likely bring back memories of his family's traumatic experience. Mario was a strong person and one I knew I could count on as we asked for his help. I also hoped it would be a way for Mario to "win one" against the evils of this type of group who so mercilessly persecute innocent people.

In just a few minutes, my cell phone rang again with another call from Mexico. I handed Mario the phone. He held it up to his ear with a shaking hand. I understand Spanish reasonably well, but when native speakers speak to each other, they speak so rapidly it's hard to catch where the conversation is going. Mario quickly left me behind.

Mario put down the phone when the line went dead and looked over at me. "Apparently, if any one person in the U.S. sends more than $1,000 to any one person in Mexico, that transaction is tracked. They don't want to have any of this tracked, so they are going to send us the names of people who will receive the money. Each person on our end can only make one transaction. Each person on their end will receive only one. They are sending the first seven names and addresses to your phone on WhatsApp. We need to go to Western Union with seven people and get the first group of transfers sent, or they are going to hurt Bob. I know these men—these animals. They will do what they say and more. We need to do what they say, and we need to do it quickly."

I could sense this was an emotional experience for Mario by his level of seriousness. Mario shared with us that they told him they were going to send Bob's head in a black plastic bag if we didn't do exactly as they instructed us to do. There was no question Mario believed them. Even though the Western Union office is ten minutes down the street, Mario told them it was actually an hour and a half away, trying to buy more time. They told him, "You have one hour before we take off his head."

It wasn't long before the WhatsApp program on my phone chimed an alert, notifying me I had a message. The message contained the names and contact information for seven people to whom we could send money through Western Union. They indicated more would come shortly, but this got us started.

We quickly gathered seven people, including the owners of our company, Mario the Spanish speaker, a couple members of the management team, and Trevor. We went to the local grocery store, which had a Western Union office inside, and prepared to send the money.

Now, if you've never sent money internationally, you might think it's a simple matter of giving them the money, telling them who gets it on the other end, and leaving. But you'd be wrong. With as much paperwork as there is, you'd think you were asking them to send their money, not yours.

They handed each of us a very lengthy form. They weren't about to send the money until they knew each sender's entire life history, or so it seemed. But even more troubling than the onerous form to fill out, there it was—right at the very top of the form. We each had to enter our name, home address, home phone number, cell phone number, and a host of other personal information.

I'd hate to say that was a deal breaker, but, quite honestly, I didn't want some drug cartel member somewhere in Mexico, or an accomplice in Salt Lake City, to have all my personal information. There's absolutely no question we all wanted to help Bob. We all love him like a brother. But when we saw we were about to put not only our lives on the line but the lives of our families, you can imagine there was a pause.

"Can't we just use a dummy address?" one of the people asked.

"No," the clerk replied. "We have to verify the address with your driver's license."

"There's no way around this?" someone else asked.

"No way whatsoever. The information on the form needs to match the information on the identification."

Our only hope was that the FBI could convince Western Union it would be acceptable for us to send the money with a falsified address and phone number. We called them. They were willing to talk to Western Union.

It was now eleven o'clock in the morning. We had been at this for nearly three hours. We'd been to the bank, we'd checked with the hotel and airline, we'd talked to both the police and FBI, and we were standing at Western Union trying to get the money sent. But from the perspective of the cartel, we had done nothing, and they were getting very angry.

Then the cartel member called my cell phone.

Speaking to the Mario, he said, "This is ridiculous. What in the world is taking so long? If we don't have the first installment here in half an hour, we're going to start cutting off Bob's fingers one by one until the money arrives."

The countdown had begun. The clock was ticking.

CHAPTER SEVENTEEN

PAYING THE RANSOM

11:00 A.M.
FRIDAY MORNING
WESTERN UNION OFFICE
SYRACUSE, UTAH

SHAWN'S STORY

THE GUILT I HAD FELT AT FIRST CONTINUED TO GROW throughout the day. I couldn't imagine how I could face Bob's wife and children if something happened. It would be bad enough to lose this great man because I'd sent him into harm's way. But to have to face his wife and children at the funeral was a thought I couldn't begin to bear.

And then it hit me like a bolt of lightning from the cosmos—Bob's family hadn't been told about his situation yet. I felt like I wanted to throw up. Wave after wave of nausea engulfed me as I thought about calling Bob's wife. Bob and his family had been close friends of ours for years. His wife was such a kind and gentle soul. How could I just call her and say, "Oh, by the way, I sent Bob to Mexico and now he might be killed"?

With everything else on my plate at the moment, I couldn't make the call. I wanted to. I just didn't think I could do it. I talked to some of the people I was with to see what they thought about letting her know. Some thought it was better to just wait until we had more information. But I knew in my heart Lynnette and the kids needed to be told—and it needed to happen sooner and not later.

I knew Bob's wife was in Idaho Falls visiting their daughter while Bob was in Mexico. I was trying to figure out how to get the information to Bob's family without doing it over the phone. It was at this point I realized that I did not have Lynnette's phone number. We didn't have a lot of time. Then I remembered meeting Bob's son-in-law a couple of times, and I thought, *I'm going to call Derik, Bob's son-in-law, and have him deliver this news in person. Nobody should have to hear this kind of news over the phone.* Derik has a friend who works in our office, so I called him to get Derik's number.

When Derik answered, I realized just how unprepared I was to tell him what was going on. What do you say? How do you tell someone? The anxiety that had been building in my soul for the last hour or so reached a point that I could barely talk.

"Derik, this is Shawn. I need to have a serious conversation with you. You need to sit down. I need to tell you something serious that's happened to Bob." With that somewhat clumsy introduction, I told Derik everything we knew. I asked him if he knew where Bob's wife was and if he would be willing to tell her what was going on. He was.

The thing that surprised me most about Derik was how calm he was. His words to me were soft and soothing, and I realized I had made the right choice about who should tell Bob's family. Derik was a rock, and I knew he would handle it perfectly. With that confidence from our conversation, I laid the burden squarely on his shoulders and turned my attention to getting the ransom paid.

The Western Union office closest to us was in the next little town inside of a Smith's Food King grocery store. We called Trevor's cell phone and had him meet us there.

While I was busy working out the details, I hadn't noticed the pain building inside me. I had had a minor surgical procedure done the night before, and the doctor had instructed me to stay down Friday, Saturday, and Sunday. I had only come into the office for just a very few minutes to take care of a couple things that needed to be done. I was planning on being there an hour or so at most and then returning home to lie down. I had felt pretty good in the morning, so I didn't see any reason not to go into the office.

And while I had been busy, I hadn't noticed the pain so much. But now, driving to Western Union, I realized it was catching up with me. The pain was definitely increasing. But what could I do? Truly, there's nothing I wouldn't do for Bob. I couldn't just leave him there. How could I say to my dear friend, "Oh, I'm sorry. I was in pain, so I went home to lie down," especially when the entire thing was my fault.

When we arrived at Western Union, Trevor was waiting for us. He had the money and was ready to pay the ransom. There was just one problem. I had been on the phone with the FBI, and they were on the way, but they'd instructed us not to pay the ransom until they got there. I thought, *Well, we don't need to send it until they get here, but we can have all the paperwork done so we can send it as soon as they arrive.*

That's when the burden I had been carrying grew exponentially. We were told we had to use our personal information to send the money. What a dilemma! I had a dear friend in Mexico who was about to start losing body parts if we didn't send the money, but how could I put all of my employees at risk by asking them to give their personal information to known killers? I couldn't ask them to provide their personal information. Frankly, none of us really wanted to.

The only person I had control over was me. I knew, as scary as it might be, I would do whatever it took. If I had to change phones, fine. If I had to sell my home and buy another, okay. I would do whatever was required. I filled out the form.

About that time, my phone rang, and Mario took the call. The look on his face said it all. He looked like he was going to be sick. I was afraid he might pass out. He looked like he had seen a ghost. I knew something was wrong. But like last time, he was speaking Spanish to the people on the other end of the line so rapidly I couldn't follow the conversation.

When he hung up, he said, "That was the cartel. If the money's not there in thirty minutes, they are going to start cutting off Bob's fingers one by one until it gets there."

This was the most delicate part of the negotiation. The FBI, which had yet to arrive, had instructed us to stall. And we had stalled as well as we could. But the fury of the cartel was rising exponentially. They kept threatening to send the *bolsa negra*, the black garbage bag with Bob's head inside, if something didn't happen immediately.

About that time, my phone buzzed, indicating an incoming message on WhatsApp. It was a photo. There were several men standing around a man tied to a chair with a black bag over his head, shoulders slumped, head bowed. It was a pitiful sight. If that was intended to strike fear in our hearts, it worked.

I knew Bob's only hope was for me to put that form—with all my personal information—up on the counter with the cash and get it sent. I knew full well the FBI might not approve, but I felt I had no choice. Desperate times called for desperate measures. This was one of those times. I laid my form and $950 on the counter and told the clerk to send it.

CHAPTER EIGHTEEN

PRAYERS FOR MY COLLEAGUES

11:00 A.M.
FRIDAY MORNING
FIESTA INN HOTEL
CHIHUAHUA, MEXICO

FROM THE TIME I GAVE SHAWN'S CELL PHONE NUMBER to my captors, the conversations they had with me were limited. Like they had done during the night, they would come on every three or four minutes or so and ask if I was there. I would respond yes, and they would again mute their end. I assumed they had turned their attention to Shawn, but I had no way of really knowing that.

As time passed, they became more and more agitated. The money wasn't making its way to Mexico like they wanted. Frankly, I couldn't imagine what was happening. I mean, really! How hard could it be? You get the money from the bank, you go to Western Union, you send the money. Problem solved. I couldn't understand how there could be a holdup.

And yet, in my heart, I knew what the problem might be, and I didn't like it. I didn't know if people in my office had ever used Western Union to transfer money. I had. I knew there were complicated forms to fill out. And I knew Western Union didn't send anything to anyone without the sender providing personal information like name, address, home phone, and business phone, all of which needed to be verified by legal identification, like a driver's license.

As I thought about it, I didn't know what I wanted most. I knew I wanted to find a way out of this mess, but I was certain I didn't want anyone I worked with to put their lives and the lives of their families in jeopardy by providing these animals with their personal information. I could easily see, in my mind's eye, Shawn or Trevor not hesitating to put their personal information down and sending the money. I knew they would do anything to secure my release, but it just couldn't happen that way. It couldn't. There was no way I could communicate any of this to them, but I prayed they would seek some alternative solution before they put their own personal information on a form that would be visible to these horrible people.

When I really stopped to think it over—as rationally as my starving, sleep-deprived body and emotionally tortured brain would let me—I knew my coworkers, my friends, had my back. That was the good news. And it was the bad news. If something happened to any of the people in my office because of this, I would never be able to forgive myself.

Each time my mind circled back to thinking *What is taking so long?*, I hoped the delay was because they were doing everything in their power to find a solution that helped me while still preserving the anonymity of everyone who would be sending money.

The seconds turned into minutes and the minutes to hours as I prayed with all the energy of my heart that God would help them find an acceptable way to help me.

When they had first announced they were holding me for ransom, a seed of hope had been planted inside me. When we had come up with a plan to transfer the money that seemed so simple and easy, I felt that hope pushing up through the dark soil of despair. But as time passed and nothing seemed to be moving forward, that fragile plant had grown so parched it was beginning to wither. Maybe there was no alternative solution. I didn't know.

CHAPTER NINETEEN

THE FAMILY

10:30 A.M.
FRIDAY MORNING
HOME OF FAMILY
IDAHO FALLS, IDAHO

MY COMMENTS

WHEN YOU'RE IN THE MIDST OF DIFFICULT TIMES, you have a tendency to see things through the lens of your own difficulties. But through all the trauma I felt personally, I had nearly constant anguished thoughts about how my family and friends were taking the news and how they would react when it was all over. I was sure they'd been told by now that I had been kidnapped, and I had prayed they would receive peace from the Holy Spirit.

Like the last couple chapters, I'm not going to try and relate the struggle of my family and friends secondhand. I'm going to let my wife share how my family reacted to the news of my kidnapping and how they contributed to my release.

LYNNETTE'S STORY

I GUESS OUR FAMILY'S STORY BEGINS IN IDAHO, where three of our four of children and their families were living. While Bob was traveling, I had gone to be with my oldest daughter, Jessica, who had experienced a late-term miscarriage the previous week. It was about ten thirty in the morning, and we had decided to take her two little boys to the zoo. We had just finished buckling them into their car seats and were about to leave when my daughter's cell phone rang.

"It's Derik," my daughter said to me as she answered the phone on speaker.

"Hi, honey," she said cheerfully to her husband.

"Are you with Lynnette?" he asked.

"Yes," she said. "We're just leaving to go to the zoo with the boys. Why?"

"I have some news you both need to hear. Are you stopped?"

"Yes," she replied. "We're still in the driveway. What's up?"

He was very calm, his voice soft and soothing, as he began.

"First, let me say we don't have a lot of information, but from what we do have, we know that Bob's okay."

As I listened to Derik and my daughter's conversation, my heart sank. I wondered what had happened. Time slowed. In that millisecond between when he had said, "Bob's okay" and when he started to explain what had happened, my mind had already played out a million scenarios. But oddly enough, I hadn't explored the scenario he was about to explain.

"Bob's being held for ransom in Mexico. His office in Utah is doing everything they can to get the ransom paid and get Bob released. They've called the FBI and are awaiting their arrival. That's really all we know right now."

With that announcement from my son-in-law, my whole life changed. Everything that was important when I had gotten in the car shifted immediately to the back burner. My husband had been kidnapped. Wait. Had Derik said "kidnapped"?

No. He'd said "held for ransom." Same thing. Bob had been kidnapped. That was my new reality.

That made zero sense to me. Trying to get my mind to focus was like wading through waist-deep molasses. Bob wasn't a soldier, a politician, a diplomat, or some wealthy financier—you know, the kinds of people this sort of thing happens to. No. Bob sold onions for a living. And when you go down the list of people who might possibly be kidnapped, people who sell onions for a living are at the bottom of the list, not the top. Don't get me wrong. I adore my husband, and everyone who knows him considers him a great man. He's just not part of the demographic that has to worry about being kidnapped.

Both my daughter and I had several questions for Derik before he hung up. But the answer was always the same: "We don't know. I've told you everything I know. You can call the office, but I don't think they know any more right now either." That seemed to be the answer we got when we called Bob's office—not because they didn't care but because that was the truth. There just wasn't any information available. We wanted to know more. Our friends and family felt the same, but there just wasn't very much information available to anyone. And, of course, when you don't have information, your mind starts making things up. And that's where you start going crazy.

My daughter looked at me, and I looked at her. We were both starting to cry. Later, people asked us if we fell apart. My answer is always the same. We didn't. Not because we were so brave or anything like that. We were simply so shocked by the news we couldn't believe it. We had no frame of reference on which to base our feelings or reactions, so the only reference you have is the movies. Thankfully, the only kidnapping most of us will ever encounter is in the movies. And movies are a poor substitute for real life.

I told Jessica, "We need to say a prayer right now."

We told the little boys that something bad had happened to Papa and we needed to say a prayer for him. They both folded their arms and bowed their heads. Even as rough-and-tumble little boys, they knew how to approach their Heavenly Father. In that prayer I poured out my heart to my Heavenly Father like I had never done in my life. I love my Heavenly Father. I say my prayers morning and night and have since I was a little girl. But never in my life have I prayed with such sincerity and intensity.

I told Heavenly Father of Bob's plight, though I was sure He already knew. I told Him what a great man Bob was and of all the good he does in the world. And again, I'm sure He already knew that. I told Him how much we, as a family, loved Bob and how much we relied on him to guide our family. I recounted to my Heavenly Father the scripture stories of men who had been bound in unfortunate circumstances and miraculously saved, like Shadrach, Meshach, and Abed-nego from the Old Testament. And finally, I pleaded with Him that if there was any way possible, that He would bless our family with the miracle of Bob's release.

I knew God was capable of granting that miracle. But I knew equally as well that if it was Bob's time to return to heaven, there would be no miraculous ending. I didn't want to pray for anything that wasn't according to God's will, so I closed by indicating we were willing to accept whatever He thought was best and by asking that His will be done.

We were already in the car, and so we drove to see my second daughter, Tiana, who worked just a few minutes away. I didn't want to tell her what was happening over the phone, so we drove to her office and asked her to come out to the parking lot and talk to us for a moment. We shared the news with her the same way Derik had shared it with us. When Tiana went back into the office and explained what was happening to her dad, her boss told her to take the rest of the day off and go be with her family. She called her husband, Travis, to join her at my oldest daughter's home.

After we left the office, we called our son, Kevin, who was a student at BYU–Idaho, about thirty minutes away. We informed him of the situation with his dad and asked him to come with his wife, Mikayla, to be with the family in Idaho Falls.

Once we got back home and all our children and their spouses had arrived from school and work, we talked about what we could do. I told my children and their spouses, "The only thing we can do is pray." So, once the family was gathered, we knelt and offered up another humble, heartfelt prayer.

I say prayer was the only thing we could do, but really prayer is the very best thing to do. This situation was like those so many people face. Not specifically, of course, but figuratively. For example, we're all going to have trials and tribulations we can't fix on our own—things completely beyond our control. Knowing we can turn to God and that He will hear and answer our prayers brings more peace during troubled times than anything we can do otherwise.

After we offered our family prayer, I made assignments to the family to call everyone we knew to ask for their prayers for Bob. I felt that if our prayers as a family were good, getting as many prayers as possible in his behalf would be even better. One daughter called my side of the family. The other called Bob's side. My son called former work colleagues. I called people Bob had served with in the church. Some were leading congregations of thousands of people. We asked everyone we called to please offer up prayers in Bob's behalf.

After calling everyone we could possibly think of and having them call everyone they could possibly think of, and so on, things got pretty chaotic. My phone rang constantly. People were devastated by the news and wanted to know more. Unfortunately, in the absence of any real news, we were going forward on faith. There wasn't anything I could really tell them except thank you.

Throughout the afternoon, calls and texts of support continued to roll in. Even people I didn't know well let us know they were praying for him. When it was all said and done, there were literally hundreds—maybe thousands—of people praying for Bob.

I was humbled that people I didn't know well were willing to pray for Bob's release. But as it turned out, people who didn't really know Bob knew of him. They knew of his reputation, of the good he had done in the community and in the world, and that was enough. It wasn't just members of our church who prayed for him. I know Jewish families who prayed for him. I know Catholics who prayed for him. I even know of those who struggle with their faith in God who agreed to offer up a prayer "just in case." I was overwhelmed both by the terrifying situation Bob was in and by the tremendous outpouring of love for him in his hour of need.

As lunchtime came and went, only the little boys could eat. None of the rest of us had an appetite. All we could do was imagine Bob's plight. As time lagged between calls and texts, I found myself trying to picture what Bob was going through. He was my "man of action" and was always quick to take care of things, solve problems, and make them better. He was so strong, vibrant, and larger than life. I remembered several instances where Bob had narrowly escaped death while traveling for work. On one hand, my mind was telling me this was just another adventure in Bob's charmed life, yet on the other hand, I also had a creeping doubt that this occasion might be different and beyond Bob's ability to fix.

It was about 1:00 p.m. when I realized, *We are all gathered here uniting our faith and prayers for Bob, but we have inadvertently left out a member of our family.* Our youngest daughter, Shayla, was serving a proselyting mission for our church in Southern Utah, and in the mad rush to contact everyone we knew, we had not gotten in touch with her.

For those who don't know about missions in our church, missionaries leave their homes for a year and a half to two years to teach people about Jesus Christ. Missionaries are tightly focused on the work in which they are laboring. They don't call home except on Christmas and Mother's Day. They don't call and talk to their friends. They don't listen to music, go to the movies, or hang out. They are literally 100 percent immersed in the work of helping people find Christ. (Note: Since our daughter's mission, changes in policy do allow missionaries to call home weekly.)

Because of that, I was concerned about distracting her from her mission. On the other hand, if something were to happen to her dad and she hadn't had the chance to unite her faith and prayers with ours, I knew she would be devastated. I decided to call her mission president and let him determine the best time to inform her of her dad's situation.

The mission president didn't even hesitate. He felt our youngest daughter needed to be included immediately. So he gave her the news and asked her to unite her faith and prayers with those of her family and friends in her dad's behalf.

At that time, our daughter had been assigned to serve on the Dixie University campus in St. George, Utah. She later told me that upon hearing the news, she immediately began looking for a more private place where she and her companion could kneel to offer a prayer for her dad. The only secluded place nearby was the dugout on the baseball field. They walked over to the dugout, and with a quick look around to ensure they were alone, she and her companion entered, knelt, and acting as voice, our daughter offered one of the most sincere prayers of her life.

I suppose that, like in any sporting venue, there had been many prayers offered by athletes in that dugout. But I'm certain none of them came close to matching the intensity of the prayer my daughter offered on behalf of herself and her companion on that hot afternoon in St. George, Utah.

Our daughter later told us that by the time she'd said amen, she had received a witness in her heart that her dad would be fine. They had then stood, left the dugout, and gone back to work. Oh, that it had been that easy for the rest of us. This was clearly a tender mercy for our lovely missionary daughter.

As time went on, it got harder and harder for the rest of us to cope. When we first got things organized, we didn't have time to think deeply about what was going on. We were too busy. But as things slowed down that afternoon, the burden got heavier and heavier as minutes turned into hours.

This was the man I loved. And I loved him like no other. I had pledged eternity to him, and we were well on our way to creating a marriage that would last throughout the eternities. We had a wonderful family together, and they were all doing so well. We loved our children and their spouses. We loved our grandsons. We were as close to one another as any family could be. And the thought that it might all be coming to an end gripped my heart like an icy fist trying to squeeze the very life out of me. I couldn't even imagine life without Bob. I didn't want to imagine it. I loved him too much to even consider life without him.

Once again, like so many times on this day of terrors, I had nowhere to turn but to my Heavenly Father. I went to the only place I could go—my knees. Only He could fix this one. Words are incapable of describing how desperately I prayed He would do exactly that.

CHAPTER TWENTY

INVOLVING THE FBI

11:45 A.M.
FRIDAY MORNING
WESTERN UNION OFFICE
CLINTON, UTAH

MY COMMENTS

THE NEGOTIATIONS FOR MY RELEASE AND THE PAYMENTS to try to bring it about continued throughout the morning and into the afternoon. I'll let Shawn explain what happened when the FBI arrived at Western Union.

SHAWN'S STORY CONTINUED

LAYING THAT CASH AND THE FORM with all my personal information on the counter was the hardest thing I've ever done. The decision wasn't hard—but the actual execution was. The realization that I'd passed through a one-way door from which there was no return settled on my shoulders like a hundred-pound weight.

It was interesting that although there were seven of us at the Western Union office, there was very little discussion going on. I'd told the group to go into the store and get something to eat, but nobody was hungry. We were all there together, drawing support from one another, and yet it was like we were there alone—each of us lost in our own thoughts.

My thoughts alternated between wondering how Bob was enduring this horrible nightmare and berating myself for having put him in this position. I was going through a kaleidoscope of emotions, one morphing into the next. I was angry—angry at the kidnappers, angry at myself, angry at what the world was becoming that something like this could happen. Then I was sad—sad for my dear friend's suffering, sad for my own suffering, sad that there were people in the world who would do such a thing to a good man. Then I was grateful—grateful Bob hadn't been killed outright, grateful there was something I could do to help, however small it might be, and grateful for a Heavenly Father who loved us all, kidnappers included, whom we could turn to. And then I was back to angry. It was a terrible, inescapable emotional roller coaster I had been thrust onto against my will.

It was about this time the FBI agents arrived at Western Union and rescued me from my thoughts and emotions. Two agents, a male and female, walked up to the counter and introduced themselves. The man was dressed about like you'd expect for a field agent for the FBI. He had on khakis and a button-down shirt. If you didn't know from the clothing he was FBI, the sunglasses would have given it away—mirrored aviator sunglasses. The woman wore a plain blouse and a skirt.

Words really can't express my relief at their arrival. I guess I didn't realize how heavy the burden had actually been until they showed up and part of it was lifted. I had been consulting with Trevor, and the two of us were doing the best we could. But we were like two blind men walking down the street holding hands—neither of us knowing where we were at, where we were going, or how we were going to get there. But there we were, walking resolutely forward in the dark.

To have someone there who had experience was a tremendous relief. Right off the bat they made it plain they weren't there to make our decisions for us, but at least they knew the rules of the game and could explain to us what our options were. That was a huge step forward from where we'd been.

We were just in the process of bringing them up to speed on everything that had happened since we'd last spoken when the woman at the counter announced my payment hadn't gone through. There was an error, apparently, and the payment had been rejected.

I was panic-stricken. I looked at my watch. Thirty minutes had passed since I'd sent the money. I knew that since it was rejected, Bob was going to start losing fingers. The FBI was trying to get me to calm down, but I all I could see was my friend with bloody stumps where his fingers used to be. I felt sick and was in agony at the thought that I had let my friend down.

I was short with the woman behind the counter as I frantically tried to get the form corrected and resent. However, she didn't know exactly why it had been rejected and had to call Mexico to find out. While she was on the phone, all I could see was Bob losing one more finger, and then another, and another. I was living in a horror movie.

Trevor asked the FBI agents if there was a possible way to send money without sending personal information to the cartel in Mexico. The male agent laid his badge and ID on the counter and told the woman she had to allow the money to be sent without requiring personal information due to the danger it imposed. She reluctantly agreed. In that moment, all seven of us present started frantically filling out new forms with bogus personal information in preparation for sending the money.

It was about that time the phone rang. The FBI agents instructed Mario to put it on speaker so they could listen.

They hadn't told us they spoke Spanish, but they must have, or they wouldn't have wanted to listen in. Mario answered the phone on speaker, and the kidnapper began to unload on him.

"Do you think this is a game?" the kidnapper thundered over the phone. "Do you think we're not serious? Do you doubt the reality of our intentions?"

While we had all been filling out our forms with the fake personal information, the woman behind the counter had been talking to Mario about the failed transaction. So when the kidnapper began his threats, Mario had the answer.

He said, "We know this is no game. We sent the money exactly as you outlined. The problem is on your end. The address you gave us doesn't exist. If you give us the correct information, we are prepared to send the payment again immediately."

I felt a wave of relief wash over me. Not only had the problem not been on our end, the form with my personal information had never made it to the kidnappers. And now, thanks to the FBI, I had a chance to change my real information for false information. What a blessing.

With a few angry words I didn't understand, the kidnappers put us on hold. When they returned to the line, they had the corrected information. We input the new data into the form and sent it straightaway. They had their first installment just before 1:00 p.m.

"So, what are our options now?" I asked Trevor and the FBI agents.

"Yeah," Trevor echoed. "What are the next steps?"

The male agent, who had been looking down, looked right into my eyes and said abruptly, "Now we wait."

That's it? Now we wait? Wait for what?

The female agent was somewhat more gentle. "We don't have any real legal jurisdiction in Chihuahua and, as you've experienced, it's difficult to get anything done from here. What would really be helpful is if we had someone working from the inside. Do you know anyone in Mexico?"

Duh. Why hadn't we moved on that? We had growers and contacts all over Mexico and along the border in Texas, and many of them were very influential people. In fact, I had been having impressions all morning that I needed to start contacting these influential people. I guess I'd just been too busy to listen. I turned to Trevor and talked it over with him. He agreed the answer was to start calling through our list of contacts to tell them Bob was in a bind in Chihuahua and to see if they felt they could help. In all honesty, what we were looking for was someone who had influence with the cartel. If someone could convince the cartel it was in their best interest to let Bob go, we'd have everything we wanted. It was a long shot, but we felt we had to try.

We started calling our contacts in Northern Mexico and along the border, and we had people at the office start calling. Surprisingly enough, we had only called three or four of our contacts when we hit pay dirt. I called a trusted grower—whose name had been on my mind all morning—named Enrique. Enrique "knew some people who knew some people." He agreed to make a few calls and see what he could find out.

That was the first glimmer of hope I'd had all day. I knew the chances that we could make something happen from this angle were razor thin, but we went for it. My prayers instantly shifted to include that Enrique, our influential friend, would be successful.

If Bob's captors were happy to get that first payment, you would never know it. They were back on the line with Mario within minutes, wondering where the rest of their money was and why it was taking so long. Taking our cue from the FBI agents, we agreed to send the rest when we knew that Bob was okay.

Within a few minutes, Bob was on the line and asked to talk to me.

"Shawn, I'm okay. I haven't been hurt and I'm alive, for the time being, but you have to know these people are serious, and if you don't get this money to them right away, I'm going to be killed. Do you understand that? What's taking so long? Is it so hard to go to Western Union and send the money?"

Did Bob think we were stalling? I could sense real concern in his voice. If only we could have simply called a time-out and talked, just the two of us, I would have been able to explain everything we had been doing and all of the challenges we had faced in actually getting the money to Mexico. He would have been able to share his fears and concerns and everything he knew, and we would have better understood each other. But there are, obviously, no time-outs in a situation like this. You just play it the best you know how and hope everything will work out.

"Bob, we are honestly doing everything we can on this end. The money is on the way."

With that, the kidnapper was back on the line and speaking in angry Spanish. I handed the phone back to Mario again.

"What about the next payment?" the kidnapper demanded.

Mario looked at me. I nodded and signaled the woman at the counter to send the next one.

"It's on the way right now," Mario told him.

That started a back and forth over the next thirty to forty-five minutes with the cartel. We would send one payment of $950, and upon receiving confirmation they'd received it, we'd send another payment. The payments were being sent to different addresses scattered over a hundred miles.

"You know," said the male FBI agent, "we've been sending a lot of money. We need to slow this process down a little bit. We need to tell them we need proof that Bob is okay before we send any more money."

After some discussion and between the third and fourth payments, he became adamant we ask for another chance to ensure Bob was okay. So the next time they called Mario, we asked to talk to Bob again.

It wasn't long before my phone rang again. It was a Mexican number. When I answered, it was Bob.

"We want to make sure you are okay," I said sincerely, wanting to ask for more details and to know for certain he was surviving this mentally, emotionally, and physically.

"I'm okay, you guys. Just get them their money." He sounded desperate.

"It's coming," I told him. "Just hang on. But we needed to make sure you're still okay."

"I haven't been hurt. I'm okay for the time being. Just get them what they want."

Like always, the line went dead, and we were left to our thoughts.

We talked about our options and tried to make sense of what was happening. It was then we got a call back from our contact in Mexico.

"Shawn, it's Enrique. As I told you earlier, I know some people who know some people who supposedly have contacts in the cartel. I started putting out feelers when you first called me. Here's what I found out. Apparently, someone in the cartel has checked throughout their system, and they swear they don't have Bob. In fact, they were furious someone else was using their name for this. I'm not exactly sure what is happening, but it sounds like the wheels are turning on their end. Granted, what I heard was thirdhand, but it sounds like they will have their people out beating the streets, looking for answers. And even more encouraging, it sounds like they are in the process of making calls to influential people in the government and the federal police to help them find some answers."

Had I heard right? The cartel wasn't involved in the kidnapping? And they were actually going to help find Bob? It would be an understatement to say I was absolutely incredulous. But then again, when the cavalry is coming, you don't judge the color of their uniform. You just pray for them. Nothing had actually happened yet, but at least we had another small sliver of hope. Things were looking up—at least a little. Weren't they?

Upon hearing this, the female FBI agent jumped into the conversation. "Our counterparts in Mexico have been alerted, as well as the US embassy in Mexico City, but they haven't had much luck in getting the wheels to turn. They are still working their end, and we are working ours."

"Wait," I said. I thought you didn't have jurisdiction in Mexico."

"We have offices there with agents who are allowed to do investigations. They just don't have legal jurisdiction," she said. "Meaning they couldn't arrest anyone."

We made the fourth payment and stepped outside on the sidewalk in front of the Smith's Food King to get better cell reception. We were all checking our phones and updating colleagues when a call rang through on my cell. It was a Mexican area code, so I interrupted the call I was on and answered the incoming call.

It was Enrique.

"You're not going to believe this," were the first words out of his mouth. "I have some news you're going to want to know about."

With that, he gave me news that almost filled my eyes with tears and drove me to my knees, right there in front of the grocery store.

CHAPTER TWENTY-ONE

THE POLICE

1:00 P.M.–3:30 P.M.
FRIDAY AFTERNOON
FIESTA INN HOTEL
CHIHUAHUA, MEXICO

THROUGHOUT THE NIGHT, I HAD RESIGNED MYSELF to the fact that I was going to be killed. I had made my peace with my Maker, and I was ready. The only questions then were *When would it happen? How would it happen? Would I be able to die with dignity, or would I be stripped of even that before I was released from this world?*

I was lost in my thoughts when my captor broke back in.

"We are going to have you call your guy in Utah," they informed me. "They want verification you're okay. Don't try anything stupid, or we will kill you before you even finish the call. You will tell them you're okay, and you will hang up. Is that clear?"

I indicated I understood and dialed Shawn's number on the disposable phone I had purchased at the convenience store there in Chihuahua. I heard his phone ringing on the other end of the line.

The call was short. Shawn asked if I was okay, and I indicated I was. That was about the extent of it. I tried to convey the sense of urgency in getting the money to Mexico, but there really wasn't time for that. I did my best.

When I say the call was short, it really was. But I suppose even if it had been an hour long, it still would have been too short. I needed more time with that friendly voice on the other end of the line. I needed some encouragement. I needed some sort of moral support. Of course, that was the thing my captors were intent on depriving me of. And thus far they had succeeded.

I looked at my watch—1:25 p.m. I contemplated a bullet passing through my skull. I prayed to have the image removed from my mind. Suddenly I was transported from that hot, musty hotel room in Chihuahua, Mexico, to the top of Grand Targhee Ski Resort in Alta, Wyoming, where we often skied as a family. My mind played the scene as clearly as if I were there right then. I got off the chairlift with my wife and followed her to the top of the run.

Lynnette's parents had been ski instructors before she was born and had instilled a love of skiing in all their children. Lynnette was a graceful, lithe skier and had beautiful form. I loved skiing with her. We had established the tradition of going skiing almost every Saturday; one, because we both loved skiing and, two, because we could go as a family, and we wanted to create memories with our children.

We waited for our son and daughters to get off the chairlift behind us and join us at the beginning of the ski run. As we waited we could hear their laughter and good-natured teasing. It was fun to see each of their skills develop over the years. Our youngest daughter used to timidly follow the pack but had become one of the better skiers among us. She was speeding in front of our son, who had taken a quick detour to make a little jump, and now they were neck and neck, racing toward us. Spraying my wife and I with a puff of crystalline, powdery snow, they skidded to a stop next to us, laughing exuberantly. What a glorious day! After bantering about who was faster and who could catch more air, the kids pushed off the top of the run, and my wife and I followed in rhythmic, synchronized turns.

But just as suddenly as I was making turns next to my wife and children, I was back in that faded blue chair in that little hotel room in Mexico. I looked at my watch again—1:26. Seriously? 1:26? I had gone from Mexico to Wyoming, skied with my family, returned to Mexico, and only one minute had passed? How was that possible? Time was quite literally standing still. It was horrible beyond description.

Lunchtime came and went, and I realized I hadn't eaten since dinner the night before. On one hand, I was famished. On the other hand, I probably couldn't have eaten even if there was something to eat. I was drained. What I really needed most was sleep, but I didn't dare nod off. I had to be vigilant—alert to everything going on around me—to have any hope for a good outcome. That thought brought a tortured grimace to my face. There could be no good outcome. Of that I was pretty certain. I knew that even if the ransom was paid, many times victims are killed anyway just to keep them from being a witness someday.

About every twenty to thirty minutes, my captors would come on the phone in a rage. "What are those people at your company thinking? They are stalling. Why? Do they think we aren't serious? We are coming to get you. It's time to start sending pictures of your hands with bloody stumps where your fingers used to be."

"The money is on the way," I told them over and over again. "I know it. I'm certain of it."

"Then where is it?" they would snarl before putting me on hold again.

And so it would go.

Finally, they broke the silence again.

"What a sorry human being you are," they told me. "Nobody in your company cares enough about you to save your life. They're all willing to let you die. I guess we'll have no choice but to kill you."

I knew that wasn't true. I knew without any question that Shawn and others in my company would give their lives for me. I knew my family would too—without hesitation. But when you're in a desperate situation and people are constantly throwing those things up in your face, it messes with your head. You know the truth as well as you know your own name, but the adversary does everything he can to make you doubt.

It's interesting how when you hear something over and over, you become numb to it and it loses its ability to reach you. Like when your school teachers tell you if you don't get your homework in you're going to fail. The first time you hear it, you get right on it. But eventually you don't take it very seriously.

That was absolutely not the case here. Even though my captors made these threats over and over, they never lost their sting. They never ceased to bring a gruesome picture to my mind and to cause the adrenaline to course through my body. They never faded in their ability to bring me to my knees emotionally, sometimes physically. I never ceased to believe them.

It was well into the afternoon when my captors instructed me to be ready for another call to Shawn. They told me exactly what to say and to hang up when I was done. With that, I dialed Shawn's cell phone number on the phone I had bought earlier in the morning. With my convenience-store phone on speaker with Shawn and my personal cell phone on speaker with the captors, they were able to hear everything. Not high-tech by any means, but it worked.

"Hello?" Shawn answered.

"Shawn, it's Bob. Have you sent the money?" I asked, almost desperate to hear that they had.

"Yes, we've sent some payments and have received confirmation that they have received it. But before we send any more money, Bob, we need to know if you've been hurt," he replied.

"No, I haven't been hurt yet, but I'm going to be if we don't get all that money here!" I pleaded.

"We're sending the money. We just need to know if you've been hurt. I'm going to ask a question only you and I know the answer to. If you're really okay, answer the question correctly. Who was your employer when I first met you years ago?"

That was easy. "Mercer Ranches up in Prosser, Washington."

"Okay," he replied, sounding relieved. "The rest of the money is ready to go. We will send it immediately."

On that statement, I cut the connection. Did Shawn just say the money was on the way? As my mind replayed the conversation with Shawn, I felt a new glimmer of hope. When Shawn asked about my previous employer, I was reassured that they were making progress. Even though our communication was limited to the brief sentences my captors allowed, Shawn had been brilliant in using an inquiry that allowed me to give a coded response and at the same time receive his hidden message that he was concerned about me and doing all he possibly could. Something was happening. I hoped he had found the type of solution I had been praying for. If he had, one way or the other this would be over soon—for all of us.

I went back to my thoughts. Inside my head was a place I didn't want to spend time, but it was the only place I had to go. Once again, waiting there for me was a giant circle of questions, each with no answer—playing over and over again to the point I thought I'd go insane. Had they found a solution? Would the cartel really let me go? Would I see my wife and family again? It was almost a welcome break when my captors would come on the line to threaten and intimidate me because at least during those moments I was free of my thoughts.

I was deep in thought when the house phone on the bedside table in my hotel room rang. My first thought was, *Why is the hotel phone in my room ringing? The only people that know I'm here are on the other line.*

Out of habit, I went over and picked up the phone.

"Bueno?" I said.

The deep Spanish voice on the other end of the line asked a question I wasn't prepared for.

"Are you Robert Meek?"

"Yes," I replied without even thinking, and the line went dead.

My captors were aware of the conversation and were shouting on the cell phone immediately. They had heard my side of the conversation because I had the cell phone on speaker.

"Who was that?" they demanded.

"I don't have any idea," I replied honestly.

"You told them your real name, didn't you?" they snarled.

Time stopped on that question. *Do I tell the truth, or do I lie?* It could have been one of their men in the lobby testing me. That man could be on his way up the stairs to kill me right this minute. I had been instructed never to divulge my real name to anyone. I was told I would die if I did. I had violated that rule, and I was pretty sure they knew it.

"Yes," I replied to my captors, sure they already had figured it out. "I gave them my real name. But look," I said, "it was an honest mistake. I replied out of habit. I'm sure nothing will come of it. I'm sorry. I won't let it happen again."

With that, there was an explosion of profanity of the other end of the line. Of course, I couldn't see them, but I knew they were literally foaming at the mouth over what I'd done.

"You're going to pay for what you've done, and you're going to pay dearly" was the invective on the other end of the line.

I had been standing while speaking on the hotel phone, and with the threat, I returned to the worn blue chair in the corner and sat down, my head in my hands. My mind was racing. Had I just signed my own death warrant without even thinking?

That whole scenario of a man testing me from the lobby was fresh on my mind when a knock came at the door. It was reinforced in my mind by the promise from my captor that I was going to pay dearly. I was almost certain whoever was at the door was here to kill me. I couldn't do anything. I couldn't even move.

Somehow I finally gathered enough strength to force myself out of the chair and to take very slow steps toward the door, robot-like. I felt like a dead man walking. As I took each step, I looked at my fingers and wondered if this would be the last time I saw them attached to my hands. They had threatened to cut them off so many times I could see bloody stumps where my fingers used to be. All night long I had felt I was going to be killed. Apparently that moment had finally arrived.

When I was within sight of the door, I wanted so badly to know who was on the other side of it. My heart sank as I realized this was an older hotel and there was no peephole. I had no idea who was on the other side of the door, but I had to open it. As I reached out to take the door knob in my hand, I thought, *I've got a 50 percent chance something horrible lies beyond that door. But on the other hand, I've got a 50 percent chance something good is there.* The truth is, I really never had much of a choice. I had to open it.

I forced my hand to lift the chain. If I'm going to be killed for acknowledging my own name, I'm ready. I've taken all the emotional abuse and terrorism I'm capable of. If by some miracle it is the police, they'll rescue me. If it's not, this will all be over when I open the door.

This was the breaking point. One way or the other, it would be over in the next few seconds.

I willed my hand to stop shaking long enough to unhook the chain from the door. I put my hand on the knob, took a very deep breath, and gave it a turn. I opened the door a few inches to peer out. There were two men and a woman standing in the hallway. One man was dressed in jeans and a maroon golf shirt with an insignia over the pocket and a Mexican flag embroidered on the arm. The other was dressed in a button-down shirt with the hotel logo on it and a tie. The woman was dressed in what appeared to be a business suit.

"Robert Meek?" the man in the golf shirt asked.

I stood frozen. For some reason the story of a young girl from Utah, Elizabeth Smart, who had been kidnapped, leapt into my mind. I remembered hearing that when they found her, they asked, "Are you Elizabeth Smart?" She had been so terrorized by her captor she couldn't respond.

My mouth went dry. I wanted to speak, but nothing would come out. I stood, staring from one of them to the other. If this was a test and I failed it again, it would be the moment of my death. You truly can't imagine the trepidation I felt at this moment. Had I come this far only to be killed in this dingy hotel? Or was this the biggest miracle that had ever occurred in my life and I was being rescued? I could barely stand from exhaustion. I had been terrorized with no sleep and no relief for . . . hours, I guessed, but it felt like days, months even. The whole ordeal had come down to this.

Feeling a deep sense of resignation, I gathered what courage I could muster and responded to the question. "Yes," I said, finally. "I'm Robert Meek."

The man in the golf shirt reached into his pocket. *This is it,* I thought and braced myself.

From his pocket, he produced a badge instead of the gun I had been anticipating.

"We're the federal police," he reaffirmed. "We're here to help you. You have to trust us."

I didn't know whether I could trust them or not, but I didn't have a choice. I looked down at the cell phone in my hand and pointed to it. Then I moved my fingers across my throat, indicating that the people on the other end could kill me. I mouthed the words "Bad men."

The woman officer quickly snatched the phone out of my hand and cut the connection. When she did that, like a bolt of lightning, an incredible surge of fear went through my body. I had protected that call so carefully for the last eighteen hours, I was sure the simple act of cutting the line would bring a horrible end upon all of us.

Suddenly, almost immediately, it rang again. The female officer powered down the phone.

"What things do you have here?" she asked kindly and gently.

"My phone, the phone I bought here in Mexico, and my charger," I replied.

"Gather everything up, and let's get out of here," she instructed me.

I gathered up my things, but I didn't dare leave the room—even with them leading the way. I had been brainwashed to believe there were men in every hall, every corner of the lobby, who, upon seeing me, would shoot to kill. Even if these people were the police, I didn't believe they could get me out alive.

"Please get your guns out before we leave," I pleaded with the officers. "There's going to be gunfire. They have me surrounded. Their men are everywhere."

"Don't worry," the woman said. "We've checked the whole place, and there's nobody here who isn't supposed to be."

But to allay my fears, they unsnapped the holsters concealed inside their jacket and shirt so they could get to their guns more quickly.

With the man and woman from the federal police on either side of me and the hotel manager in front of us, we walked down the hall and into the elevator. Words can't describe the terror I felt walking down the hallway. There was a blind corner at the end by the elevator, and I was certain someone would jump out and I'd be a dead man. They kept trying to walk forward, keeping me between them, and I kept trying to hold back. The brainwashing had been so complete that even standing between two armed police officers, I was in mortal fear of my life.

Shockingly, at least to me, we got into the elevator without incident. For just ten to fifteen seconds I felt safe. Then the elevator doors opened to the lobby. I had already had some terrifying and traumatic experiences in two different hotel lobbies in the last eighteen hours, and this one was every bit as bad as my last ones had been.

I was gripped with complete panic. My eyes raced around the room, looking for potential killers. But with the officers flanking me, the hotel manager walked over to the desk, and we walked calmly—or rather, they walked calmly, while I walked like a robot—across the lobby, out the front door, and directly into the unmarked car sitting only three feet from the door.

It was a bright, sunny day, and very hot, just like it always is in Chihuahua. The sun felt good on my skin as I waited for the officers to unlock the door. Unlike last night when I'd arrived, the streets were now filled with traffic as the city approached rush hour.

On one hand, I felt immense relief being in this old RAV4 with the *federales*. On the other hand, I knew this could be a setup. I knew the badges these people had shown me could be bogus and they could be taking me out of town to torture and kill me in a quieter place. But somehow I felt okay with them. Or, better said, I felt good about them in my heart, and, quite frankly, I didn't have room in my heart for anything else to fear. I left with the agents. The hotel manager stayed in the hotel. As I rode through the streets of the town with the officers, I began to feel relief that perhaps this apparent rescue might actually be happening. I had been through so much that in my mind I wanted to believe it was real, but I still had my doubts.

I was still very uncomfortable with the police car. Yes, it was unmarked, so it didn't draw attention to us. But it was almost derelict. It was a twenty-year-old Toyota RAV 4, and only two gears in the transmission worked. Our top speed could only be twenty-five to thirty miles an hour. My head was on a swivel—turning, waiting, and looking for a car to come racing up alongside us and fill the broken-down Toyota with bullets.

As we drove through the city, my anxiety slowly started to subside. When I finally realized I had actually been freed, I told the woman officer, "I need to call my wife. I don't want to use my phone because if they have it bugged, they might be able to track me from the call. Could I use your phone to call my wife?"

The woman smiled and quickly handed me her personal phone.

With my fingers shaking so badly, I almost couldn't make them go to the correct numbers, but I lovingly pressed the buttons to the number I knew so well. Tears were streaming down my face as the line connected and began to ring on the other end.

"Hello?" It was Lynette. Her voice was tentative and uncertain. She sounded tired and afraid.

"Lynnette, it's me," I said through my tears. "I'm with the police in Chihuahua. I'm okay. I've been rescued, and I'm coming home."

"Is it really you?" she asked incredulously. "Are you really safe?"

"I am safe. I'm with the police. I don't want you to worry. I will call you back as soon as I can. If something happens in the meantime, anything at all, I wrote you a note in my scriptures that's tagged to my favorite verse. Go read that. It will give you some idea of what's been happening. And one other thing—I don't want you to be alone. Gather the family around you and keep them there. I've got to go. I love you, Lynnette. Don't be afraid."

On the other end of the phone, I heard Lynnette's voice break with emotion as she said through her tears, "They're all here now. I love you, Bob."

My wife had answered her phone on speaker. Quickly followed by my wife's affirmation of her love for me, I heard my daughter Jessica say, "Dad, I love you"; then my son, Kevin, "Love you, Dad"; then my other daughter Tiana, "I love you, Dad."

I said, "I love you guys too. I will call again shortly. Everything's going to be fine. I will see you soon. I love you!"

CHAPTER TWENTY-TWO

GLORIOUS NEWS

3:30 P.M.
FRIDAY AFTERNOON
HOME OF FAMILY
IDAHO FALLS, IDAHO

I'M GOING TO LET MY WIFE AND MY BUSINESS PARTNER share how the news of my release affected my family and my coworkers.

LYNNETTE'S MEMORIES OF RECEIVING THE GOOD NEWS

THROUGHOUT THE DAY, WHENEVER A NEW family member joined us, we would kneel once again and pour out our hearts to our Heavenly Father. We had all grown up reading the scriptures, and we knew very well the power of prayer. We had read the stories of biblical prophets who had been spared in their hour of need because of their prayers and the prayers of others.

But having read the scriptures, we also knew that if it was your time to go, Heavenly Father wouldn't intervene—not because He didn't care or wasn't aware, but because it was your time or it fulfilled some necessary aspect of His grand plan.

The intent of our prayers was not to overpower God's will, by any means. Our intent was to seek a blessing at His hand if it was His will to provide it.

After talking to Bob's coworkers several times and spending a great deal of time on the phone with the FBI, I felt like I was going into shock. By the time I finished with the FBI, my hands were shaking so badly I could hardly hold the phone. I had received all the support I could imagine from friends and family, but I was still carrying an enormous burden alone as well.

Throughout the day my phone had been ringing off the hook. People I knew well, people I didn't know well, and people I'm not sure I knew at all called to wish me well. They let me know they would pray nonstop for my husband and that they would do anything necessary to lighten my load. I was amazed and humbled at the outpouring of love from all corners of my life. I can't tell you how many well-wishing texts I received. It was truly amazing.

There really wasn't much we could do as a family besides wait and pray. While we were waiting and chatting quietly, my son got on the internet to try and find out more information about Chihuahua. What he found was not encouraging. The state department had an advisory for that area indicating travel there was extremely dangerous. They listed kidnapping as a very real danger.

As he looked further on the internet, he found out there were several kinds of kidnappings. There was the kind you see on television, where they take you somewhere and hold you. That was the only kind I was aware of. But then he found a discussion of "virtual kidnapping," where the victim is held by phone and never sees his captors. I had never heard of anything like that. Apparently evil is as creative as good, which I had never before considered.

Finally, my son came upon the statistics for those saved versus those killed. I don't remember the exact percentages, but I recall the likelihood of being rescued as minuscule. At that point, my son put the computer away. Sometimes it's better not to know.

We watched social media pretty closely for news regarding the kidnapping. We didn't know how internet-savvy the kidnappers were, but we felt that if there were rumors going around Facebook, it could do Bob more harm than good. We explained those fears to some of our well-meaning friends who had posted in an effort to get more people praying for Bob. They understood and promptly took the posts down.

Ever since the ordeal had begun for us at 10:30 in the morning, we had run nonstop—talking to friends and family and doing everything in our power to help from our end. Mercifully, there hadn't been time to stop and really ponder what was going on. I'm grateful for that. But as the afternoon wore on, we had a little time to wonder what was going to happen.

Many people have asked me if I had premonitions or feelings that everything would be okay and that Bob would be coming home. The answer is no. As mentioned, our missionary daughter Shayla later told us she had had a powerful spiritual peace wash over her when she found out. But the rest of us weren't as lucky. Much to the contrary—although we were praying for a miracle, we all had to admit we might never see Bob again in this life. Things were pretty somber around my daughter's house that day.

But by saying that, I wouldn't want you to think we had lost faith. We were all praying with a faith we had never found before. The truth is, not having that assurance allowed us to continue to pray with an intensity that wouldn't have been possible, or necessary, if we had known Bob would be coming home soon. I am certain those intense prayers had an impact on the outcome of the whole situation. I'm grateful that our family and friends never weakened in the intensity of the prayers they offered in Bob's behalf right up until the end.

We were sitting in the living room when my phone rang. I looked at the caller ID: "Mexico."

My heart stopped. What if the kidnappers were moving from negotiating with Bob's work to negotiating with me? How would I handle that? What would I say? With tremendous trepidation, I answered the phone with speaker on so those around me could hear.

On the other end of the line was a voice I knew well—a voice I had been wondering all day if I would ever hear again in this life. It was Bob!

"Lynnette, it's Bob," he began. "I've been rescued. I'm with the police. Everything's going to be okay. I don't want you to worry."

From the first word, I knew it was Bob. There was no question about that. But with the movies as my only reference, I could see Bob sitting in a chair on the other end of the line with a kidnapper's gun to his head, telling him exactly what to say. I was waiting for the other shoe to drop. I didn't know exactly what to say.

"Are you really okay?" I asked.

"You have to trust me," he said. "I'm on my way to the police station right now. But there's one thing I need you to know. I'm pretty sure I'm going to be okay. But if for any reason something happens, I wrote you all a note in my electronic scriptures attached to my favorite scripture. Go and read it. It will help you to understand what's happened over the last eighteen hours. I've got to go. I'll call you back as soon as I can. I love you." Bob later told me that he felt stress talking on the phone with me during his ride to the police station. He didn't want to be distracted by talking too long on the phone as he looked for what could have been drive by shooters.

Before he hung up, I said, "I love you, Bob."

Since the children had all been listening in on the speaker, before their dad could hang up, they chimed in, "Love you, Dad. "I love you dad." "We love you, Dad." It was probably the most emotional moment in all of our lives.

After looking at the statistics, we knew there was nothing short of a miracle that would bring Bob home to us. We knew that without intervention from on high, we would never see Bob again in this life. We sat in stunned silence, knowing we had just seen the hand of God moving in our behalf. It was miraculous. It was incredible. But most of all, it was humbling. It brought all of us to our knees, and intense prayers of gratitude poured from our hearts to our Heavenly Father, much the same way—moments before—blessings from heaven had been poured out upon us all.

My first thought was to call Shawn, Bob's partner. They had been working tirelessly on this since first thing this morning, and I knew they would be as excited and as grateful as we were.

Shawn's Experiences When the Rescue Was Announced

We had sent four installments of the ransom and were awaiting more names to be able to send more. We had just stepped outside on the sidewalk in front of Smith's when the phone rang. It was Lynnette.

"Bob's been rescued," she gushed. "He's with the police right now."

I'd had such a feeling of foreboding all day long, I asked, "Are you sure he's really safe?"

"Yes," she said. "I'm pretty sure, why?"

"I don't know. I've just had such a horrible feeling all day."

"Well," she said, "I've been pretty concerned too, and there was one thing he said when he called that concerned me. He said, 'If anything happens to me, anything at all,' I should read a note attached to his favorite scripture. If he's free, why would he say 'if anything happens'?"

We both agreed we'd feel a lot better when he was on the ground in Utah.

I hung up the phone and told everyone, "Bob's been rescued. He's with the police, heading to the police station. He should be home tonight."

With that, the sober, almost somber mood in front of Smith's changed to elation. We were high-fiving each other and giving hugs all around. It's hard to imagine what people thought as they left with their groceries. Here was a group of adults acting like high school students who had just won the big game. We didn't care. If they were staring, we didn't even notice them. This was a moment never to be forgotten. A miracle had occurred for Bob, and we were ecstatic.

All of a sudden, I realized Trevor had run back into the store. He was gone for several minutes and then came back.

"Where did you go?" I asked.

"If Bob's free, we needed to cancel payment on the ransom," he said matter-of-factly.

Trevor's a thinker. I really like that about him. We were all basking in the moment, and he was saving the company thousands of dollars. It turned out one of the payments had already gone through. But the other three were still waiting pickup. We got those back. So what did the kidnappers get for their trouble? $950.

Everyone there was rejoicing. I was feeling good, but there was still that ever-present concern gnawing at my gut. Why wasn't I over the moon? I mean, I was happy, but I just wasn't feeling the unbounded joy everyone else seemed to be feeling.

It was then I noticed the two FBI agents. The male agent had been on the phone for the last several minutes and announced to the group that he had just received a call from the federal police in Mexico informing him Bob was indeed with them. But he was still pretty stoic. I asked him what was up. His reply was right out of a classic police drama.

"For us it's not over until our counterparts in Mexico tell us it's over. We have a confirmation from one source. That's indeed good news, but the rejoicing will have to wait until our people confirm what we think we know."

That news seemed to bring everyone down a bit, but not for long. If Bob said he'd been rescued by the police and the police said they'd rescued him, we were pretty excited. We knew it was Mexico. Anything was possible. But after nearly seven hours of constant bad news, the good news felt pretty good.

About that time, the phone rang. The call was from Mexico, only this time it wasn't from the number we had been receiving calls from. I took it anyway.

"Shawn?" Bob said after I answered the phone. "It's Bob. I've been rescued. I'm with the police."

I put the phone on speaker so everyone could hear.

"I'm going to the police station to make a report, and then I'm coming home."

"Are you really free?" I asked.

"I'm really free. Trust me. Everything is going to be fine."

"Are you okay?" I asked. "I mean, did they hurt you?"

"No, I'm fine. I'll tell you all about it when I get home. I've got to go. I'll be in touch soon."

Hearing Bob's voice with my own ears was somehow better. There's no question Lynnette was telling me the truth. She is as honest a woman, as near perfect a woman as there is. It's not like I doubted her on any level. It was just somehow reassuring to hear my dear friend's voice.

But even after hearing his voice, the uneasiness I had been feeling all day simply wouldn't leave. I wasn't sure why. I had been comforted by the call. We had all rejoiced that our friend had been rescued. Things were going way better than we could have ever reasonably hoped.

But it wasn't all lollipops and rainbows.

What happened next completely baffled me.

CHAPTER TWENTY-THREE

THE LONG ROAD HOME

3:30–9:30 P.M.
FRIDAY AFTERNOON / EVENING
FEDERAL POLICE STATION
CHIHUAHUA, MEXICO

WHEN WE ARRIVED AT THE FEDERAL POLICE STATION, the agents parked across the street and down the block a ways. While my anxiety had been settling down during the car ride, I was suddenly on high alert. We were going to get out of the car, walk down the sidewalk, and cross the street. Now, when you normally cross the street, you don't think about it, you just do it. But in the nightmare I had been living for the last eighteen hours, they had convinced me beyond all doubt there were cartel members on every corner, behind every bush, hiding in every doorway, whose sole purpose in life was to kill me on sight. I wasn't sure I wanted to chance it. I couldn't very well stay in the car, but I didn't dare get out—even with an armed police officer on each side of me.

When we had pulled up to the station, I was tremendously disappointed to see that there were no parking spaces in front of the building. I don't know what I expected in a huge city like Chihuahua. But what I wanted more than anything was to pull up to the building, park on the sidewalk, and jump from the car to the door of the office. But it wasn't to be. We had to park across the street and down the block.

Although I was desperately afraid of getting out of the police vehicle, I knew that it also wasn't safe to stay inside it. If I could just get into the police station safely, I would be fine. So I left the vehicle, walking between the officers. While we crossed the road, my eyes darted to and fro like a madman. My paranoia level was at DEFCON 1. Was a drive-by shooter just waiting for the perfect moment to zoom in and open fire? My autonomic nervous system kicked in and pumped my body full of fight-or-flight chemicals. Even though I'd grown up pretty scrappy, there would be no fighting here. I was ready to flee with all my strength at the slightest provocation.

It wasn't until I was inside the police station that I really began to feel safe. I guess, on some level, I realized there was nothing in there that could or would hurt me. I knew police stations in general were pretty heavily fortified if something were to happen. And once I was there, I finally started letting my guard down.

To say my mind was full would be a huge understatement. For eighteen hours I had been resigned to my death—resigned that I would never see my wife and children again in this life. And now, in the last fifteen minutes, I had talked to both my wife and my business colleague. It looked like I was going home. But, like anyone in that situation, I had seen enough movies to know how quickly it could all change. I wouldn't be truly safe until my feet were planted on Utah soil. I had tasted the possibility of "life" again, and I was willing to do whatever it took to bring that to pass.

I can't tell you how good it was to talk to my wife. I know that some people have difficulties in their marriages and that maybe talking to their spouse after such a traumatic experience wouldn't be so wonderful. But our marriage is as near perfect as you can get.

Like I always do, I felt a lift from just talking to her. I was tired. I was terrorized. I was beyond exhausted. I wondered if I could take another step. But after hearing her voice, I knew I would have as much energy as I needed to return to her. It was a miracle, really. There's no other way to describe it. I had witnessed—no, been part of, been the recipient of—an incredible miracle.

I was taken to the office of the supervisor of the two detectives who had rescued me. I was introduced to him, and they left. He and I spent over an hour together while he had me recount every detail I could remember. He was kind but very thorough. Instead of making me uncomfortable, it gave me peace that he had examined my case so carefully.

When we finished, I went back to the front of the station and, to my great surprise, there sat Enrique, one of our contacts from Chihuahua whom I had known for years. He was one of the people who helped us source onions in Mexico.

"Hey, Enrique. What are you doing in here?" I asked.

"Getting you out of trouble," he said with a grin. "But right now I'm here to help you take whatever the next steps are."

The female officer who had rescued me gently interrupted our reunion. "Can I ask a favor of you?"

"Of course," I responded. "Anything at all."

"We'd like to get a picture with you. This is absolutely the best day of our career."

When I asked why that was, she said, "We don't usually rescue people. We recover them." She could tell I didn't completely understand, so she clarified, "We don't rescue living people. We recover dead bodies."

I still didn't understand. "If you normally recover bodies, how did you find me?" I asked.

"Easy," she said. "You wrote the address of the new hotel in your planner and left it on the desk by the phone. All we had to do was go to the address in your planner and ask about you."

"But I didn't register under my own name," I countered.

"No," she said. "But you did use an American name. We asked if Robert Meek was staying in the hotel, and they said no. So we asked if there were any Americans in the hotel, and they led us to you. We asked if you were Robert Meek, you said yes, and here we are."

Once again, I was humbled. It brought home, on an entirely different level, the miracle I'd received. What if I hadn't left my planner in the room? What if it had been closed instead of open to the right page? What if I had used the Mexican name to check into the Fiesta Inn hotel instead of the name of my stepfather? What if, what if, what if. Little things I had done, obviously at the unseen or unfelt promptings of the Holy Spirit, had led to my rescue. Again, looking back, I can see the hand of the Lord moving in my experience from the beginning to the end. Nothing could possibly be more humbling than that!

Enrique took a picture of the three of us together, and we gave each other heartfelt hugs. Then they said, "Well, I think we're done here. You're free to go anytime."

Free to go? Where would I go? Outside? With evil men on every corner? I said, "I need to get back to the States."

"I doubt there are any flights to the States at this hour," the female officer replied. It was just before 6:00 p.m. "You might get a flight to Mexico City and then from there to the States."

I turned to Enrique. "Let's make some calls before we leave."

CHAPTER TWENTY-FOUR

LOGISTICS

4:00 - 7:00 P.M.
FRIDAY EVENING
SYRACUSE, UTAH

WHILE I WAS WITH THE POLICE IN MEXICO, Shawn and Trevor were busy in Utah trying to do what they could to get me home as quickly as possible. There was also a flurry of activity in my family.

Shawn's Story

It was probably around 5:00 p.m. when the FBI agents got the call from their counterparts in Mexico confirming Bob's release.

With that, we said our goodbyes and headed back to the office.

Even with a positive confirmation from the FBI in Mexico, I was still being crushed by the burden of having sent my dear friend and colleague into harm's way. Try as I might, I couldn't shake it. The long and short of it—I was responsible. I had sent him there, and something bad had happened. Yes, he was free of his captors for the time being. But who was to say he wouldn't be captured again? He was still in Mexico, and as long as he was in Mexico, he was at risk.

I knew I wouldn't really be able to feel peace until Bob Meek was standing on Utah soil next to his lovely wife and children.

I told Trevor, "I think we need to do whatever it takes to get Bob home as quickly as possible. What do you think?"

"I agree. What are you thinking?"

"I think we need to find someone with a plane to fly him home."

Trevor said, "We should at least see what's available in commercial flights. I'll get someone checking on flights out of Chihuahua, and you start calling around and see what you can do about a private plane."

The office confirmed my fear that there were no more commercial flights to the United States for the day, so that was out. Bob might be able to connect through some other city in Mexico, but that was unacceptable to me. I wanted him out, and I wanted him out now!

I started calling everyone I knew who had a private plane to see what it would take to go to Chihuahua to get Bob. It turns out that to take a plane into Mexico, you have to have Mexican insurance. It was past closing time, and there was no way to get insurance until the next day. That effectively killed the possibility of going to Mexico to pick him up.

So I started calling to see if we could find someone who could pick Bob up in El Paso. But even that proved difficult. I was still trying to find someone when Enrique called. He said, after talking to Bob, he was going to take Bob to the airport in El Paso. He also indicated they would work from their end on trying to find someone to pick Bob up there.

I asked Enrique why Bob was coming with him to El Paso. I mean, weren't they sending some sort of armed guard to escort him out of the country? Weren't the police going to take him? Why was Enrique taking him?

Enrique explained that the police had told Bob, "You're free to go."

I about fell off my chair. Free to go? Like he had been hauled in for a traffic violation or something? Free to go? Alone? Hello?!? He was in one of the most dangerous cities in the world, certainly in Mexico, he had just suffered a horrific kidnapping, and he was free to go? I couldn't believe it. My jaw hung open. Free to go—by yourself—wherever you dare. I couldn't believe they were washing their hands of this. It was the craziest thing I'd ever heard.

With the knowledge they were sending Bob on his way with no escort, I became more and more frantic to find Bob a way home. With every call I made and every negative response I received, I became a little more panicky. I had to get Bob out of Mexico. That was all there was to it. There was no other acceptable outcome. I had to get Bob home, and it had to be today. I knew Bob would never feel really safe until he got home. I knew that because I knew I could never really rest until Bob was safely home.

About 6:00 p.m. I got a call from Bob. He had called someone he knew in Idaho Falls, Idaho, and they were going to send a jet to El Paso to pick him up and bring him to Ogden, Utah. Perfect. Now the only major challenge in front of us was to make sure he got from Chihuahua to El Paso without incident.

With everything planned and the pieces seemingly falling into place, we called it a day. Trevor and I had returned to the office to work on this whole thing from there. We decided that all we could do now was go home and wait. That was the hard part—waiting. But we had done all we could. It was in God's hands now. I told Trevor how grateful I was for his help and jumped in my truck to head home. He did the same. We were the last two to leave the office.

Arriving home, my wife reminded me that we had been planning to go watch my nephew's football game in Salt Lake City. He was the star quarterback on his team, and we had been trying to get down there and watch him play. I told her we should go. I travel enough that I'm often not home when he plays. I've learned over the years that when a chance to do something you want to do presents itself, you'd better take it. So we drove to Salt Lake.

Although my body was seated in a stadium with thousands of screaming football fans, my spirit was in the back seat of a pickup truck somewhere in the Mexican desert with Enrique and Bob. I was praying nonstop that everything would go smoothly on the ride home. I knew the dangers on the road between Chihuahua and El Paso. We were so close to getting Bob out of Mexico. I couldn't let anything happen now, and yet there was nothing I could personally do for him. Only God could help him now. I prayed that He would.

4:30–8:30 P.M.
FRIDAY EVENING
IDAHO FALLS, IDAHO

LYNETTE'S STORY

PEOPLE OFTEN ASK, "WEREN'T YOU JUST OVER THE MOON when you got the call that Bob had been rescued?" My answer is always the same. We weren't. In fact, we took the news of his release about the same way we took the news of his capture—with some sense of disbelief and shock.

I suppose I shouldn't have been shocked or surprised. We had been praying for a miracle for Bob. Hundreds, maybe thousands, of us had been praying for his release. And now he was free. Why should I be shocked when that's what we had been hoping for, that's what we'd been praying for, and that's what had happened?

I knew in my heart it was the prayers of thousands of people that had saved Bob. There was no doubt in my mind.

There is great power in prayer. There are those who will attribute Bob's release to luck or happenstance, but we know the truth. God hears the prayers of His children, and He answers those prayers. I was so grateful He had answered ours.

After we knelt and expressed to God our profound gratitude for the miracle that had just taken place, we realized we needed another miracle. We found out Bob would be driving to the border with Enrique, and we knew that road was probably the most dangerous road in Mexico. The thought that Bob might somehow become entangled with the real cartel was more than I could bear—more than I could bear for myself, and more than I could bear for him. That started our intense prayers for his safe passage from Chihuahua to El Paso.

The first thing we did after offering our prayers of thanksgiving was to begin calling everyone we had asked to pray and informing them that Bob had been rescued. There was a tremendous outpouring of love and tears of gratitude from our friends and family. Like we had, everyone knew the odds of Bob getting out alive. Everyone recognized the miracle that had just occurred and rejoiced with us in God's mercy. And all agreed to keep praying for Bob's continued safety until he got home.

Once we'd called everyone, I told my family, "Dad's going to come to Utah. We need to go down there so we're there when he comes in." And with that, we loaded into three cars and headed south.

It was on the way to Utah we got a call from Bob indicating he'd arrived in the United States. We knew that El Paso was on the border and was somewhat more dangerous than some cities, but he was much safer now than he had been just a few hours before. He had made it through Ciudad Juarez without any problems. He was in the USA. We were only a few hours from seeing him. My heart leapt. For the first time since this whole thing began, I started to feel safe in the thought that I was actually going to be able see him, hold him, and express my love to him again.

The feelings of gratitude that were washing over me like waves on the seashore were so powerful my eyes filled with tears. Bob was safely back in the United States. He was coming home. I can't tell you how good that sounded. When you've braced yourself for the worst, you're totally unprepared for the best. That was certainly the case with this.

So off to Utah we went, nobody really talking much—each of us lost in our thoughts. Though we were all together in our cars, it was a very personal, very private moment for each of us. I'm not sure how it can be that way; I just know that it was. There we were, thinking, praying, and feeling so blessed. It was good to be close to those we loved and to feel that support, even if we didn't talk very much.

If you're looking for a way to tell someone what a family is, I'd say that's the definition of family. We can work and play and laugh and live together in a very boisterous way, but we're just as comfortable being with each other without any of those things—quietly supporting each other and feeling one another's support.

CHAPTER TWENTY-FIVE

DEADLY PATHS

6:00 P.M.
FRIDAY EVENING
FEDERAL POLICE STATION
CHIHUAHUA, MEXICO

ENRIQUE AND I CALLED SHAWN AND HAD PEOPLE in the office start looking for flights. We called the airport and started looking ourselves, but it was pretty grim. The only way to get out of Chihuahua at this point was to fly to Mexico City, spend the night in a hotel, and fly out the next morning. The idea of staying in another Mexican hotel sent my level of anxiety through the roof. There was no way.

"There must be some other way," I said. "What about a private plane?"

Unfortunately, getting private planes in and out of Mexico on short notice is much more difficult than you'd imagine. There are insurance issues, the need to prefile a flight plan when customs and immigration are available, and all kinds of other things.

"I can take you to El Paso," Enrique offered. "Surely you could get a flight from there."

The thought of driving to El Paso sent a shiver up my spine. It would be dark before long, and because of the cartel activity, the road from Chihuahua to Ciudad Juarez, which lay on the Mexican side of the border across from El Paso, was one of the most dangerous roads in Mexico in daylight.

Many people have asked, "Why did you do it? Why didn't you just go to Mexico City? Wouldn't that have been safer?" The answer, of course, is yes, it would have probably been safer. But you have to understand my state of mind. I hadn't slept in nearly forty hours. I hadn't eaten in nearly thirty. And during that time, I had been dragged through the depths of hell. I had taken all I could take. Emotionally, there was no way I could sit for hours in an airport, waiting for a plane. I couldn't go to a hotel and check in.

No. I needed to be out of Mexico and back on U.S. soil as fast as humanly possible. I knew my Heavenly Father had provided a miracle in freeing me from my captors, and I had to believe He would keep me safe until I got back home. I really had no other choice. I had to accept Enrique's offer.

So that became the plan. I called Shawn and asked him to see if he could find a private plane to pick me up in El Paso at about 10:00 p.m. and fly me to Utah.

While we were making those plans, the officers had been talking amongst themselves. When I got off the phone, they said, "We need to go back to the first hotel and get your things."

"Forget my things," I said. "There's nothing there worth my life."

But as we talked it over, I realized they needed to see the room as part of their investigation. And they might have questions for me as they looked thing over. I agreed to go if they would accompany me.

We arrived at the first hotel I had stayed in, and my heart literally quit beating for several seconds. I had ridden over there with Enrique, while the officers had gone in their own vehicle. I saw them get out and knew that's what I was supposed to do. Even Enrique was looking at me with a look that said, "Are you getting out?"

But I was frozen with fear. Some of the worst hours of my entire life were spent in that place. I didn't know if I could go inside. But I finally summoned enough courage, opened my door, got out, and walked into the hotel.

It was eerie. I recognized the front desk clerk. I wondered if he'd had anything to do with this since he was the one who'd dispatched the bad guys on that first call last night. How would they have known I was in that room if he or someone else at the hotel hadn't told them?

I was very nervous as I walked through the lobby. Two police officers weren't enough. I should have asked for a bigger escort. I followed the officers across the lobby and into the elevator. We went up to the room, and I began putting my things in the suitcase. The room was just as I had left it. It looked as if someone had indeed ransacked it.

As quickly as I possibly could, I tossed everything into my suitcase, and we went down the hall to the elevator. When the doors opened at the bottom, I just knew there would be someone waiting for me. There wasn't. We walked across the lobby and out the front door. One look up and down the street where I had walked just a few hours before, a prisoner of the voice on my phone, and we were in Enrique's pickup and on our way.

Enrique wanted to make a quick stop at McDonalds to get a burger before we had to drive four hours. I was hungry, but wasn't sure I could eat much. It seemed like forever since I had eaten anything, but when the food came, I ate one or two french fries and one bite of my burger. Instead of nourishing me, it really just made me feel sick. I did drink some of the soda as we drove along.

The plan was to drive to El Paso. That meant we had to pass through Ciudad Juarez, arguably the most dangerous city in Mexico. There was no reasonable alternative route. I remembered hearing they'd had nearly five thousand gun-related murders in Juarez over the last few years. I had been in the clutches of a cartel. I had been rescued. And now I was racing along at eighty miles an hour, right back into the belly of the beast. I knew that most people weren't abducted from hotels in this part of Mexico; they were abducted on this road. It was four hours from Chihuahua to El Paso. Four very intense hours.

As we rode along, Enrique explained how Shawn had called him around noon Utah time and about all the things he had done to intervene. When I asked him how he had found me at the police station, he simply said, "I have my ways."

My time with Enrique bounced back and forth between conversation with him and prayer—mostly prayer. Enrique seemed to sense I wasn't really up to much conversation, and he was respectful of that. It wasn't that I didn't want to share with him what had happened, especially in light of all he had done and was doing for me. But I was just so emotionally depleted I couldn't do it.

What I knew for sure was I had received a miracle. The police had verified it. The fact that I'd been rescued was a miracle. But I was going to need another one. Here we were, driving after dark on what had to be one of the most dangerous stretches of highway in the world. It would take another miracle to get to El Paso without being "guests" of the cartel a second time in twenty-four hours. That's what I was praying for—one more chance. My prayers were a pleading from deep in my soul that nothing would happen between here and home and that I would be reunited with the wife, family, and friends I loved so dearly.

I'd known for a long time that Enrique was connected in Mexico. Obviously I didn't understand how connected. But even with those connections, I marveled that he would risk his own life to drive me from Chihuahua to El Paso. He seemed pretty matter-of-fact about the whole thing, but I knew inside he must be as unsettled as I was on this stretch of road. I hoped he was praying for our safety too.

Talking to my wife had heightened the sense of love I felt for her, and although I was resigned last night to never seeing her again in this life, right in that moment I couldn't imagine being this close and having that torn away from both of us. My prayers were as intense in that moment as they had been at any time in the whole ordeal. I wanted to go home. I was going home. But what I really wanted was not to "go home." I wanted to "be home"—in the comfort and safety of my own house, with my own family, sleeping in my own bed, surrounded by those I love most in this world. I wanted that like I had never wanted anything else in my whole life.

Driving through Ciudad Juarez was as scary as anything I have ever done. Perhaps it wasn't that driving through the city was so scary in and of itself as much as I was so spent emotionally that every little thing seemed like an emotional mountain to climb. I knew the city was the most dangerous in Mexico, and I was imagining all kinds of scenarios as we passed through.

All I could think of was those movies where you're so close you can taste it and then it's all snatched away. I was so close I could see the lights of the USA. Oh, how I wanted to be there. I was right there. It was so important for me to be there. It took several lifetimes to finally get to the border. We parked the car, got out, and took our papers into the immigration office.

In the back of my mind, I was expecting some huge, insurmountable problem to raise its ugly head. But it was all pretty routine. They stamped our passports, and we were on our way. One more stop on the US side of the border. Again, no issues. They stamped our passports and waved us through.

Suddenly there we were—back in the United States. You would think I would be giddy, elated, out of my mind. But for some reason I still didn't feel safe. I knew the likelihood of something bad happening had gone down significantly now that we were on the US side of the border. But deep inside I couldn't shake the anxiety that kept pushing its way into my active consciousness every time I turned around.

Before I knew it, we were pulling into the FBO (where the private planes park) at El Paso International Airport. I walked into the terminal with Enrique, all my stuff in tow. There was a man sitting on the couch in the waiting room.

"Are you Bob Meek?" he asked with a smile.

"I am," I replied. It was interesting to me how much easier it was to respond this time than when the *federales* had asked me the same question just a few hours before.

"I'm your ride," he said. "Let's mount up and get you home. The plane is right out here, and it's gassed up and ready to go."

CHAPTER TWENTY-SIX

THE FINAL LEG

10:00 P.M.
FRIDAY NIGHT
EL PASO INTERNATIONAL AIRPORT
EL PASO, TEXAS

THAT SMALL PRIVATE AVIATION TERMINAL AT THE AIRPORT in El Paso will always hold a special place in my heart. Forever burned in my mind is the memory of the hug I gave Enrique. The man had put his life at risk to save mine. The Savior said, "Greater love hath no man that he lay down his life for his friends." That's what Enrique had done for me. He hadn't been required to actually give his life, but by driving that dangerous road at night, he had demonstrated he had obviously been prepared to do so.

He had put his life in grave danger. That was the bottom line. And he had done so without hesitation. I knew Enrique had a wife and children at home. I knew they loved their husband and father as much as my family loved me. I knew they wanted their dad to come home safely as much as my family wanted me to do so. The only word that describes the gratitude I have for what he did is *humbled.* I was humbled that this man had very literally risked his life for me—more humbled than I had ever been. Enrique is a hero in my eyes and will always be. How could he have done that for me? It was almost too much to contemplate.

After warm embraces, we left each other. The pilot and I carried my bags out the door leading to the jet, and Enrique disappeared into the night. And just like that, I was on my way home.

For the first time since this whole ordeal had begun, I felt safe and secure. Until now, there had always been a fear or a doubt or a worry somewhere in the back of my mind. But here I was. As the wheels of that private jet left the ground and we climbed into the star-filled sky, I felt safe. This was the last leg. I would be home with my family in just over two hours.

From my spot in the copilot's seat I could see everything. I watched the lights of southern Texas grow smaller as we climbed into the darkness. It was almost 10:00 p.m. and I was going home! The pilot pointed out landmarks as we flew along.

"See those lights over there?" he asked about halfway through our flight.

I said, "Way off in the distance to the left?"

"Yeah. Those are the lights of St. George, Utah."

I felt a warm glow fill my soul. My daughter Shayla was serving a church mission there. I wondered if my wife had told her everything that was happening. I wondered if she had been worried about me. I hoped not. The warm glow persisted. I was proud of her for what she was doing. I was proud of all my children. I always had been. I couldn't think of a time when I wasn't proud that they were my children and grateful I was their dad. I hoped they knew that. I was pretty sure they did. A deep feeling of love and gratitude filled my heart, and it also filled my eyes.

SHAWN'S STORY

WE LEFT HOME ABOUT 11:00 P.M. TO GO TO THE AIRPORT to meet Bob. This day had been the longest of my life, and I was looking forward to a happy conclusion. When I heard that Bob was on the jet, my anxiety for him decreased significantly.

Even though I had put him at risk, it was all working out. He would be home shortly, and we could put this behind us. It's a difficult thing to look back on but an infinitely more difficult thing to have been in the middle of. I hoped nothing like this would ever happen to me again.

As I drove to the airport, all I could think of was what might have been. It made me physically sick to my stomach to think about what could have happened. I was so grateful Bob had gotten out of Mexico physically unharmed. I was so grateful the tears we would shed at the airport would be tears of love and gratitude and not tears of loss and sorrow. I was grateful I would be able to face Lynette as someone who helped secure Bob's release and not as the person who had caused his death.

It was a time of tremendous introspection. I was overflowing with gratitude. Against my better judgment, I had allowed my dear friend to put himself at risk and the worst had happened. And then, by the grace of God, a miracle had happened. Bob was alive, and he would be home in a few short minutes. How different that thought was than those I had felt throughout the day. It was a great day to be alive.

I got to the airport about 11:30 p.m., and Bob's family was already there waiting. Lynnette ran toward me as I got out of my pickup. We embraced, both of us overcome by emotion and relief. All I could think about was how differently this might have turned out had something happened to Bob. The gratitude once again flowed over and around me, enveloping me in its warmth.

Suddenly I realized we were all still outside.

"The airport is locked," Lynette told me. "There's nobody around, and there doesn't seem to be any way in. There's a number you can call, so I called it. There was no answer."

"I guess we'll wait out here," I told her. "There has to be a way for them to get out. People land here at night. There has to be some way out. We'll just wait here by the fence until they get here."

And that began the waiting. It was an upbeat mood but not loud and boisterous. I think that deep, penetrating feeling of gratitude tempered our excitement and enthusiasm. Our love for God was first and foremost in our minds.

And so we waited, nervously, excitedly, anticipating being reunited with this man we all loved. Trevor and I waited off to the side. This was a family moment. We were pleased to be included.

9:00–11:30 P.M.
FRIDAY NIGHT
OGDEN, UTAH, AIRPORT

LYNETTE'S STORY

WE ARRIVED AT OUR HOME IN UTAH two or three hours before we needed to be at the airport. Never in my life had such a short time passed so slowly. Our grandsons kept saying, "Is it time to go get Papa yet?"

I would reply, "Not quite. Just a few more minutes." But I have to admit I was as excited to go to the airport as they were. I couldn't wait. And yet that's exactly what I had to do. We all did.

At 11:00 p.m., we headed to the airport. It's a small airport for such a big town and doesn't get much use with Salt Lake only thirty minutes away. We arrived in plenty of time and expected everything to be open. We figured we would go in, sit down, and wait for Bob's arrival. What we found was a locked door, no lights, and no way to get to where the planes were to come in.

With that, we took up a position at the fence, under a street light, where we hoped Bob would be able to see us when he landed. Shawn and Trevor both came. We were grateful to have them join us. This was pretty much a family gathering, but we consider them part of our family, so we were glad they were there to share this moment with us. And, after all, they had been working tirelessly all day for Bob's release. I can't imagine what would have happened if they hadn't done what they did. I don't even want to think about it.

This was a glorious reunion. I can't think of a time when I was happier to see my beloved husband. You can never have a "life-altering" experience without having your life altered. I knew I would never be the same after this.

MY STORY

AS WE GOT CLOSER AND CLOSER TO SALT LAKE CITY, I could feel the intensity building. Most of the air traffic stays west of the freeway, out over the Great Salt Lake. But since we were going north of the city, we dropped to about six thousand feet and flew right up the Salt Lake Valley along the mountains. It was a spectacular view.

But as great as the view was, I only had eyes for the landing strip. It's only three or four minutes in a jet from Salt Lake City to Ogden, but it seemed like it took forever.

I was looking for the airport when the pilot said, "Can you see the airport?"

I couldn't. Then I heard some clicks in my headset, and the runway lit up like a Christmas tree.

"See it now?" he asked.

"Wow!" I said. "How did they know we were coming?"

"They didn't," was his simple reply. "I turned on the lights by clicking the push-to-talk button on the stick. They make it possible for pilots to control the lights so they don't have to have someone attend the airport at all hours when it's not busy."

Even from two miles out, in the dark, a thousand feet above the airport, I was looking for my family. I couldn't see them. When we landed and opened the door, I still couldn't see them. I called Lynette on the phone.

"Where are you guys?" I asked, hoping they were there.

"We're over here by the fence, under the street light," she said. "The airport's locked up tight."

I started looking around and suddenly saw my son-in-law up on a large container, waving his arms. I dropped my bags and ran to them. My heart was full, and tears were streaming down my cheeks as I approached them. They were all filled with the same emotions. I couldn't believe it. Here I was—home. Home with those who were nearest and dearest to my heart. Miraculously, I had come through physically unharmed. I was home. I couldn't believe it.

I got to the fence and gave my wife a kiss through the wire. My children were grabbing my hands.

"How do we get this fence out from between us?" I asked.

She replied, "I don't know. We looked everywhere for a gate or something and couldn't find one anywhere."

By then the pilot had joined us at the fence. "Let me go see what I can find," he said. "People fly in here at night. There's got to be a way out." Within just a couple of minutes, the pilot was calling to me to join him. He'd found the way out.

I can't tell you how good it felt to embrace my wife. I hung on and didn't want to ever let her go again. What do you say at a time like that? There aren't words that begin to describe what's in your heart, so you don't say anything. And I suppose nothing needs to be said. When you've been married for over thirty years to a woman you love more than life itself, nothing really needs to be said. You both already know what the other is thinking.

When I could finally let go of my wife, I turned to my children. My oldest daughter gave me a long hug, and we broke the embrace. Then she came right back and did it again. Then again. She couldn't get enough. I couldn't either. The same with my other children. We laughed, and we cried, and we gave thanks to God for the opportunity to be able to do so.

Everyone had been totally respectful of the situation, not mentioning the eight-hundred-pound gorilla in the room. Finally, Shawn asked, "So, Bob, can you tell us what happened?"

If anyone deserved to hear what had happened, it was Shawn. Without his efforts and those of so many others, I would not have been rescued. I knew Shawn felt responsible for my ordeal—I could see it in his face—but the truth was, he had nothing to do with my decision to go to Mexico a few days earlier. The decision was mine and mine alone. His deep anguish over my kidnapping and the way he took the entire responsibility upon his own shoulders just speaks to the type of man Shawn is. He is—and always had been—a true friend.

I really did want to share the whole experience with everyone who had come to the airport. But I was so exhausted I knew I simply didn't have it in me to relive everything that had happened. So, as I sat on the tailgate of my pickup, I gave them a very short version of the story. Of course, we talked about many of the actual details of the kidnapping, but the part I focused on was the relationship I developed with Sergio that night. It was one of the most fascinating parts for me, and I knew it would be for them as well. It didn't take long to share, but it allowed them to understand more clearly what had happened, and they were very surprised to hear a part of the story they had no idea had occurred.

When I finished recounting the brief version of my story, I suggested maybe it was time to go home and get some sleep. Everyone nodded in agreement, and with that, we all went our separate ways. I was grateful to those who could be there. It was wonderful to feel their support. And I was grateful to be headed home to sleep in my own bed, with my wife and children all under the same roof.

We got home and talked briefly. Then we knelt as a family and offered a prayer of thanksgiving to our Father in Heaven for watching over me and bringing me home to the family I loved so much. I told Heavenly Father how grateful I was for each family member and how much they meant to me. I acknowledged His hand in my rescue. I acknowledged His power in keeping me safe throughout the whole ordeal. It was another very humbling experience to feel His power all around us.

Nobody wanted that moment to end. It had been a glorious reunion, indeed, but I was spent.

Tomorrow would be a better day—much better. I was looking forward to holding my loved ones and never letting them go.

EPILOGUE

I WILL NEVER FORGET THOSE EIGHTEEN HOURS. How can I? Though the memory of the exquisite pain and terror has dimmed slightly by time, the whole ordeal very literally changed my life. There were so many unanswered questions while it was all going on, and some of those still exist today.

For example, I was debriefed by the FBI when I returned home. They had a lot of questions for me, but the first question I had for them was whether they had caught my captors. They indicated that my captors had left no trace of who they were or of their whereabouts. When I wondered out loud if they had searched the cartels for answers, they indicated that these types of kidnappings were almost never cartel based. In fact, it turns out many of them are actually committed by criminals serving time in a prison somewhere. So not only were my captors not who they said they were, they were—potentially at least—never even in a position to hurt me physically.

I have to admit the thought that I could have just walked out and disappeared into the night had crossed my mind. I have been asked by many people why I didn't just hang up, or walk out, or whatever. The answer is this: you have one roll of the dice. If you're correct and you leave the hotel and escape into the night, you're free. If you're wrong, you're dead before you reach the end of the hallway. With stakes that high, would you bet your life that they really didn't have you under surveillance? I guess I'm not that big of gambler. Or said another way, I wasn't willing to risk my life on the *possibility* that nobody was really watching me.

In closing, since this happened, I've had the opportunity to share my story with many groups and individuals. As I share this with them, I have one objective in mind. I don't want anyone to think I was somehow different or better than others who have found themselves in a similar situation in Mexico. God blessed me that night and day, and I will always recognize that.

I had the opportunity to share my story with a group of young teenagers, and when I was finished, many of the youth came up and wanted to ask questions. Toward the end, one young girl observed, "Do you realize that this experience wasn't about you?" I looked at her, puzzled, thinking that I knew the characters in the experience and that if it wasn't about me, then who was it about? She said, "This experience is about Sergio. God loves all His children, and that night He wanted to get a message to Sergio but needed someone to deliver it. He knew he could trust you to deliver that message, and you did. Sergio needed one more chance and you helped give it to him."

That was a humbling thought. I suppose that sometimes our lives are about second chances. As I look back on this experience and the countless lessons I have learned, I primarily feel gratitude. If God came to me today and offered to erase my memory of this whole experience—the bad and the good—I would beg him to please let it stay. Sergio and I are the same. We all are. We all need one more chance.

ABOUT THE AUTHORS

ROBERT MEEK

ROBERT MEEK HAS BEEN INVOLVED IN AGRICULTURE his whole career. His involvement in ag has allowed him to travel to forty-eight of the fifty states in our great nation and has sent him to over twenty countries. Being fluent in Spanish has helped him build countless lifelong relationships with many of the wonderful people in Latin America. Robert resides in Morgan, Utah, where he and his wife enjoy the quiet mountain valley they call home. They are the parents of four married kids and currently have five grandsons.

ALLAN WEBB

ALLAN WEBB IS A STORYTELLER WHOSE GREATEST PERSONAL satisfaction comes from helping those who have a compelling story to tell share it with those who would benefit from it. Allan and his wife live in the mountains near Yellowstone National Park. They are parents to five children and grandparents to twenty grandchildren.

43581592R00119

Made in the USA
Lexington, KY
29 June 2019